*Civil Art: Urban Space
as Architectural Task*

Civil Art:

NAi Publishers

Vincent van Rossem

Urban Space as Architectural Task

Rob Krier
in The Hague:
The Resident

Contents

Architecture and the City 8
Berlage, Dudok, Weeber 42
Urban Renewal 56

Project Documentation
Gunnar Daan 96
Bert Dirrix 102
Peter Drijver 106
Michael Graves 112
Karelse Van der Meer Architecten 118
Rob Krier 124
Adolfo Natalini 130
Cesar Pelli 138
Sjoerd Soeters 144
CH & Partners 152

Personal Index 158
Colophon 159

Foreword

'Many generations of planners have come to grief here, but now, as a result of a remarkable combination of circumstances, the time seems to be ripe for a spatial composition that will enable a humane oasis to be built in an urban no man's land.'

Rob Krier – 1993

A fairly recent aerial photograph of the area nowadays known as The Resident shows the old buildings along Herengracht and Fluwelen Burgwal, the white top of City Hall, the building complex housing the Ministries of Foreign Affairs and Justice, the 'Black Madonna' and, in the middle of the site, the

Transitorium. Not much wrong with that, you may think, but in fact the photograph tells another story. Set against the background of a culture of urban life that has been twenty centuries in the making, it is a scene of devastation, an urban landscape that has been effectively reduced to silence. An arid no man's land, caught between two worlds, with no hint of dialogue.

Many Dutch cities contain – alas – comparable areas. So The Resident is both an ordinary and a somewhat unusual child of its time. It is an area with a curious anatomy and a rather stubborn character. Perhaps it was this very situation that prompted those involved to pursue a 'risky' form of collaboration involving workshops (now a fairly tired concept) and any other ploy that would help to establish a consultative forum. The main thinking behind this was that such complex matters are better solved in a short sharp meeting of minds than in the more customary long-drawn-out welter of words.

In addition, the project coincided with a decision to allow the 'market' a greater say in government accommodation, something that has been handled here with commendable care, with an eye to the quality of our life – today, tomorrow and the day after tomorrow. In line with Rob Krier's ideas, a competent and loyal team of designers was assembled, all of whom have worked with heart and soul on the project.

The Government, the City Of The Hague and the Project Developer – perhaps even to their own surprise and certainly to the surprise of onlookers – were quite unanimous as to the objective of the exercise: the realization of an outstanding project that might stand as an example for 'Beautiful Holland' in the next century. And, in fits and starts, people collaborated enthusiastically to ensure that it succeeded. What it came down to was inspiration, teamwork and trust. Rob Krier, Frans Evers, Peter Noordanus and Ton Meijer 'took care' of that.

Looking back from the vantage point of mid-1966, with work on the infrastructure and the buildings already underway, it is now possible to reconstruct and to interpret the events and emotions surrounding the genesis of The Resident. To show how logical the task was, or how the conflict between various urbanistic views – including those of successive generations – had to be resolved and reconciled. To reconstruct and explain how the idea of a magnificent public space gradually evolved, first in our heads, and how, later still, it began to take shape on paper. This book is a record of that history and all those who played a part in it.

A period of fifteen years separates the commencement of the BANK study and the completion of The Resident – fairly normal for this type of project but it does not make the task of evaluation and judgement any easier. This is what makes a book like this, with its precise record of facts and arguments – and the lessons they contain for the future – so important. Fortunately the author has not needed to reconstruct anything for he was usually there in person.

In five years or so, in the twenty-first century, The Resident will reveal its true character and beauty. Until then we must consult our imagination – and this book.

Kees Rijnboutt, July 1996

Architecture and the City

top: Le Corbusier, Villa Stein, Garches, 1927
right: Le Corbusier, Maisons Jaoul, Neuilly, Paris, 1952

The critical moment

In an article in the September 1955 issue of the *Architectural Review*, James Stirling discussed the Maisons Jaoul that Le Corbusier had built in Paris in the early 1950s. Stirling had just taken his first steps in the architectural profession and no one knew then that he would later become world famous. The article is in fact a comparison between Villa Stein, a house Le Corbusier had built in the Parisian suburb of Garches in the 1920s, and the newly-completed project in Paris. This comparison, Stirling realized, led irrevocably to the conclusion that a turning point had occurred in Le Corbusier's oeuvre. Villa Stein and the Maisons Jaoul, according to Stirling, 'represent the extremes of his vocabulary: the former, rational, urbane, programmatic, the latter, personal and anti-mechanistic. If style is the crystallization of an attitude, then these buildings, so different even at the most superficial level of comparison, may, on examination, reveal something of a philosophical change of attitude on the part of their author.'[1]

Stirling, who as a young architect had of course thoroughly familiarized himself with the basic tenets of modern architecture as formulated by Le Corbusier in *Vers une architecture* (Towards a New Architecture), was above all surprised by the fact that the great French master had utterly and abruptly renounced the aesthetic of modern technology that he had once advocated with so much fervour. What disturbed him was the fact that the Maisons Jaoul were conventionally beautiful – 'their sheer plastic virtuosity is beyond emulation' – in the same way as Greek temples are beautiful: '(...) it is disturbing to find little reference to the rational principles which are the basis of the modern movement, and it is difficult to avoid assessing these buildings except in terms of art for art's sake.'[2] The idea that the allegedly 'rational' principles of the modern movement were in need of critical revision was to be the source of much debate in the course of the next thirty years.

Although he did not say so in so many words, Stirling ultimately decided that from an art-historical perspective Villa Stein was more interesting than the Maisons Jaoul. The argument that led to his change

1   James Stirling, 'Garches to Jaoul', in: Carlo Palazzolo and
    Riccardo Vio, *In the Footsteps of Le Corbusier*, New York 1991,
    p. 81.
2   Op. cit. p. 90.

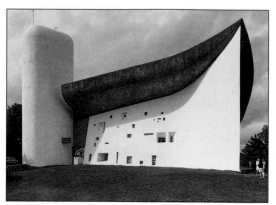

of heart is a perfect illustration of the doctrinaire nature of the modern movement. What it boiled down to was that the Maisons Jaoul were undoubtedly pleasanter to live in, still worse, one did not even have to be eccentric to be able to appreciate these houses. Villa Stein on the other hand was not so much a dwelling as a manifesto: 'utopian, it anticipates, and participates in, the progress of twentieth-century emancipation. A monument, not to an age which is dead, but to a way of life which has not generally arrived, and a continuous reminder of the quality to which all architects must aspire if modern architecture is to retain its vitality.'[3] In retrospect one can only wonder that the magic words 'technology' and 'modernity' should have exerted such a hold over even sensible people like James Stirling.

A year later and once again for the *Architectural Review*, Stirling examined the church Le Corbusier had built at Ronchamp. On this occasion he realized that the history of modern architecture had indeed entered a dramatic phase. The article opened with a reference to two buildings completed in 1952: 'with the simultaneous appearance of Lever House in New York and the Unité in Marseille, it had become obvious that the stylistic schism between Europe and the New World had entered on a decisive phase. The issue of art or technology had divided the ideological basis of the modern movement.'[4]

The church at Ronchamp, in his analysis, had little or nothing to do with the principles of the modern movement: '(...) there is little to appeal to the intellect, and nothing to analyse or stimulate curiosity.'[5] It was, quite simply, a building that appealed to the emotions, to a certain poetic sensitivity that is subconsciously present even in completely non-musical people. Although Stirling was frankly unsettled by the Maisons Jaoul and the church at Ronchamp, he was at least willing to face facts. Le Corbusier's authority was so unassailable that even his criticism of the development of modern architecture, for which he himself had laid the foundations, had to be regarded as a *fait accompli* of architectural history. He confronted the utterly impersonal perfectionism of Lever House with a defiantly personal signature. 'Certainly', wrote a bewildered Stirling, 'the forms which have developed from the rational and the initial ideology of the modern movement, are being mannerized and changed into a conscious imperfectionism.'[6]

From a historical perspective it is not so very difficult to understand that Le Corbusier's postwar work set a critical standard that disqualified in advance every lazy and uncreative interpretation of *Vers une architecture*. When Lever House was designed and built it was an authentic contribution to the development of modern architecture, which is why it also bears comparison with Unité in Marseille, but the

3 Op. cit. p. 91.
4 James Stirling, 'Ronchamp: Le Corbusier's Chapel and the Crisis of Rationalism', in: Palazzolo, Vio 1991 (see note 1), p. 215.
5 Op. cit. p. 218.
6 Op. cit. p. 231.

top: Le Corbusier, Notre-Dame du Haut, Ronchamp, 1950-1955
middle: Le Corbusier, Unité d'Habitation, Marseille, 1946-1952

right: Skidmore, Owings & Merrill, Lever House, New York, 1952

hundred thousand clones of this building that have since been erected all over the world, regardless of the local climate, culture or setting, are clear proof that technical perfectionism in itself is totally uninteresting for architecture.

With his enormous rhetorical talent as a writer Le Corbusier has often given a misleadingly simple picture of architecture in a technologically advanced society. Surely only a very cursory acquaintance with *Vers un architecture* could ever convince anyone that this was a suitable first-year text for architecture students. The ostensibly successful marriage between technology and architecture it describes must in fact

be seen as a tremendous intellectual trial of strength. On the very first page, where the themes of technology and architecture are introduced, Le Corbusier draws a sharp distinction between the engineer, who calculates, and the architect, whose work is the 'pure creation of his spirit'.[7] The precise implications of this are made clear later on using the example of the Parthenon in Athens: 'profile and contour are the touchstone of the Architect. Here he reveals himself as artist or mere engineer.'[8]

Once again, fairly logical from a historical perspective, but James Stirling's output demonstrates how difficult it was to find a way out of the dilemmas that were continually cropping up in architecture during the 1950s. After a hasty, perhaps even somewhat lazy, attempt to integrate the vocabulary of the Maisons Jaoul into his own work –

in the Ham Common apartment building in London – Stirling returned to the roots of the modern movement. His first genuine masterpiece, the Engineering Building designed for Leicester University in 1959, is a brilliant example of the lessons to be learnt from Russian Constructivism. Only many years later, with the Stuttgart Staatsgalerie for instance, designed in 1977, did Stirling finally succeed in freeing himself altogether from the doctrinaire legacy that had plagued the 1950s.[9]

The English architectural historian Reyner Banham was the first to put the problem in a historical perspective. In 1960, with his book *Theory and Design in the First Machine Age*, he showed just how fraught the relationship between technology and architecture, which Le Corbusier had described in *Vers une architecture* as a fairly simple one, had in fact been. Banham concluded with an account of the difficult choice architects had been faced with ever since. 'It may well be that what we have hitherto understood as architecture, and what we are beginning to understand of technology are incompatible disciplines. The architect who proposes to run with technology knows that he will be in fast company, and that, in order to keep up, he may have to emulate the Futurists, and discard his whole cultural load, including the professional garments by which he is recognized as an architect. If, on the other hand, he decides not to do this, he may find that a technological culture has decided to go on without him.'[10]

7 Le Corbusier, *Vers une Architecture*, Paris 1923, p. 3.
8 Op. cit. p. 163.
9 Deyan Sudjic, *New Directions in British Architecture. Norman Foster, Richard Rogers, James Stirling*, London 1986.

top: James Stirling, Ham Common, Richmond, 1955
right: James Stirling, Engineering Building (Leicester University), Leicester, 1959

Another interesting document in this context is the travel journal kept by the American critic Lewis Mumford during the three months he spent touring Europe in 1957. Mumford was not a conservative critic but he was only too well acquainted with the effects an unbridled faith in progress had had in his native country to be beguiled by much of what he saw in Europe. He pointed out that modern architecture had lost a lot of its original charm because its vocabulary, still fresh and genuinely new in 1930, had been reduced to clichés by a massive building programme. He also emphasized the extremely negative impact increased car traffic was having on the historic inner cities and lamented the less than helpful town planning effects of some types of high-rise.

Before the war, when the architecture of the modern movement consisted of a fairly small number of buildings scattered across Europe, no one had noticed the poverty of its stylistic resources. This, suggested Mumford, may have been why '(...) no one suspected that an urban quarter designed on these restrictive principles alone might be an appalling monument of esthetic dullness.'[11] A similar problem arose in town planning. The limited possibilities offered by a purely functional approach resulted in development plans in which the same configuration of buildings was repeated ad nauseam. The most ludicrous modern town planning ideas, according to Mumford, were formulated by Le Corbusier during the 1920s. These visions of tall buildings in a park-like setting may well have been in keeping with the very latest thinking on the need for light and air, but these urbanist panoramas were totally bereft of all the familiar indicators of urban space. With some surprise Mumford noted that it was precisely these ideas that were popular in Europe. 'Those plans of Le Corbusier are today, ironically, the principal holdovers of that period, perhaps because they now unconsciously symbolize the inflation of money, the deflation of human hopes, and what one must perhaps call the "normalization of the irrational".'[12]

Naturally, Le Corbusier's more recent work also figured in Mumford's diaries. The church at Ronchamp, which Mumford saw as an expression of regret, prompted an analysis of the crisis in the

modern movement. 'This repentance with a vengeance has the violence of caricature, but however the Master's more pious admirers try to disguise it, his reaction points to a serious lack in the old credo.'[13] The result was a lack of direction and confusion but this could also be viewed positively for, argued Mumford, these symptoms '(...) are due partly to a not unsound effort to reacquire some of the architectural qualities that were cast aside by the somewhat naïve formulations of the nineteen-twenties.'[14]

What especially saddened Mumford was the high-rise that had shot up all over Europe. The Roehampton Estate, a much-vaunted housing estate with tall tower blocks on the western edge of London, left him cold. Such architecture and such construction methods, he

10 Reyner Banham, *Theory and Design in the First Machine Age*, London 1960, p. 329, 330.
11 Lewis Mumford, 'Babel in Europe', in: *The Highway and the City*, New York 1963, pp. 2, 3.
12 Op. cit. p. 3.
13 Op. cit. p. 4.
14 Op. cit. p. 5.

concluded, produced an 'unpleasant kind of urban space, gigantic in scale, procrustean in feeling, empty in human content.'[15] It was a verdict that would later be endorsed by the German psychiatrist Alexander Mitscherlich in his essay *Die Unwirtlichkeit unserer Städte*.[16] As far as high-rise was concerned, Mumford made an exception for Amsterdam where planners had not lost sight of the human scale; on the other hand he was put off by the grim penny-pinching mentality he encountered in the Netherlands. Nor did he have anything positive to say about European office buildings. 'Everywhere, the glass wall, with continuous windows and opaque glass spandrels, has become fashionable, there are postwar examples as far apart as London and Geneva. But this is a dead end of glossy architectural boredom, against which a reaction is already overdue.'[17]

Finally he turned his attention to car traffic. Wherever he looked, the old market squares were full of cars, '(...) in Paris, the Place Vendôme has entirely lost its serenity and order to the parked and moving vehicles. (...) In Amsterdam the parked cars so effectively line the canals of the central city that they completely spoil the townscape.'[18] People talked about spectacular solutions, huge multistorey car parks, motorways through the city, but 'no one, it seems, pays heed to our own grim experience, which is that the more facilities are provided for the motorcar, the more cars appear.'[19] The car, according to Mumford, was an inappropriate means of transport for the city; public transport and the pedestrian should be given precedence: '(...) the notion that you can free the motorcar of all restrictions in the city without devastating the city's living spaces is a delusion that will probably cause a lot more damage before it dies.'[20]

These prophetic words were written almost forty years ago and it is depressing to have to record that nowhere has any attempt been made to avert this disaster. Quite the contrary, for the belief in a new world, with lots of high-rise buildings surrounded by motorways and parks lacking any sense of scale, was so strong that no one wanted to be bothered by prophets of doom like Mumford. Before long, *Der Monat*, the German magazine that had published his travel journal, printed a reaction from a Berlin expert. This writer, dazzled by the vision of a city free from any reference to the historic city, listed once again all the most doctrinaire arguments in favour of destroying the conception of traditional urban space. It began with the title, 'Ein neues Raumgefühl' (A New Sense of Space) that had evidently been borrowed without much thought – and without acknowledgement – from *Platz und Monument* (Square and Monument) a book, published in 1908, by the German architectural historian A.E. Brinckmann.[21] This book, however, was about the way in which urban space had been shaped during the Baroque period, using street and square façades. The space around high-rise buildings on the other hand was deliberately uninflected and totally diffuse. The argumentation therefore was entirely abstract: new international relations and space travel presaged a world without borders, ergo, the city, too, should be a borderless space where motorways and high-rise serve to remind us of the fact that the city dweller is not yet entirely extinct. 'Because of high-rise', so the argument went, 'the third dimension is now part of the experience of every resident and with it a new relationship with nature, not with the tree in

15 Op. cit. p. 7; Miles Glendinning, Stefan Muthesius, *Tower Block*, New Haven, London 1994.
16 Alexander Mitscherlich, *Die Unwirtlichkeit unserer Städte*, Frankfurt 1965.
17 Mumford 1963 (see note 11), p. 9.
18 Op. cit. p. 10.
19 Ibid.
20 Op. cit. p. 11.
21 A.E. Brinckmann, *Platz und Monument*, Berlin 1908.

Alton Estate, Roehampton, Londen

the garden of course, but rather with the wide expanse of the sky. But the inevitable consequence of this is the breaking down of boundedness, the driving back of neighbours, of the people living opposite. A high-rise that is not surrounded by empty space is a caricature, an abuse.[22] In these kinds of arguments one thing always follows from the other with inescapable logic, there are no alternatives, nor any sympathy for human experience, so that the idea that a tree surrounded by grass might be more meaningful than open skies simply does not occur, any more than the realization that people might prefer to see flesh and blood neighbours instead of anonymous specks in the distance.

'Even traffic structures', the text continued to prophesize, 'that at first sight appear to be purely technical and economic measures, serve the new structural reorganization. (...) The same applies here as to high-rise: the modern traffic structures, with their initially excessive use of cloverleafs, viaducts and underpasses, (...) have chopped up the urban terrain just as relentlessly as the huge railway terminals and shunting-yards once did; but held in check and sensibly deployed they serve to recuperate and develop our lives.'[23]

We now know that Mumford's critique of high-rise was entirely justified, while we have daily confirmation of the accuracy of his prophetic words about car traffic. All over the world postwar high-rise housing estates have fallen to the wrecker's hammer. Only recently, in October 1994, 'La Démocratie', a district of Lyons, was blown up: ten fifteen-storey tower blocks completed in 1967.[24] In fact, one tower in 'La Démocratie' had already been dynamited in 1983.[25] Research has shown time and time again that the construction of high-rise housing estates owes more to the doctrinaire tenacity of politicians than to sound urban development policy.[26] Living in high-rise apartments is only attractive when the disadvantages are offset by truly urban surroundings offering a rich mix of cultural facilities, something which is never the case in the outer suburbs.

Mumford's accuracy with respect to car use scarcely requires comment. Although the automobile has undoubtedly widened the horizon of countless millions, it is now perfectly obvious that it is impossible to grant the car free access to the city without destroying the city itself. Many practical examples bear witness to this fact, as for instance the vandalistic route (Wibautstraat – Weesperstraat – IJ-tunnel) that cuts a swathe through Amsterdam, but it had already been analytically demonstrated as long ago as 1963 in *Traffic in Towns*, a brilliant English report.[28] There are but two solutions: either cities must be radically reconstructed, or car use in urban areas must be drastically reduced. In the Netherlands a comprehensive study of traffic and transport carried out in 1972[28] likewise indicated that car use, if allowed to grow unchecked, would have serious spatial consequences, a conclusion that excited 'shock and resentment' at the time.[29]

The tragedy of the modern movement lies in its very success. This postwar success came fairly suddenly and unexpectedly and by the time it began to dawn on insiders that most of their pre-war ideas were extremely one-sided and incomplete, they discovered that modernism had acquired a momentum of its own.

22 Hans Stephan, 'Ein neues Raumgefühl', in: *Der Monat* 10 (1958) Vol. 114 (March), p. 67.
23 Op. cit. pp. 67, 68.
24 *NRC Handelsblad*, 12 October 1994.
25 Spiro Kostof, *The City Assembled*, London 1992, p. 120.
26 Maarten Mentzel, *Bijlmermeer als grensverleggend ideaal*, Delft 1989.
27 Colin Buchanan (ed.), *Traffic in Towns*, London 1963.
28 Nederlands Economisch Instituut, *Rapport Integrale Verkeers-en Vervoersstudie*, The Hague 1972.
29 *NRC Handelsblad* 7 December 1972.

In the dynamic circumstances of accelerating economic growth architects and planners lost their grip on developments. The architect Aldo van Eyck, writing in the magazine *Forum* in 1962, complained that Dutch housing construction had acquired an inhuman character under the influence of huge bureaucratic organizations.[30] The urbanist Cornelis van Eesteren, speaking at a conference in Moscow in 1958, expressed his concern about the growth of traffic and increasing environmental pollution. Yet it was already too late. There was a proliferation of architecture and town planning which led, in aesthetic terms, to a fatal form of homogenization, with the consequence that modernism's reputation was lost for good.

It is rarely fruitful to address history with questions that begin with 'if this' or 'if that', but the question whether the modern movement might have survived in a more favourable climate is nonetheless a fascinating one. Moreover, sooner or later it will be necessary to re-examine the modernist legacy that 'post-modernism' has somewhat hastily rejected in its turn. Evidence that such an investigation might produce interesting results is to be found in the oeuvre of Cesar Pelli. Over the past thirty years this American architect, trained in the office of Eero Saarinen, has designed a great many office buildings which demonstrate that the post-Lever House modernist vocabulary is still serviceable and capable of further development.

Also deserving of more attention in this context is Mumford's suggestion that the modern movement might have been more balanced and less juvenile had it subjected its own theoretical development to critical analysis. During the postwar congresses of the Congrès Internationaux d'Architecture Moderne (CIAM) there was fierce discussion as to the nature and content of this analysis. The younger affiliates in particular were perfectly aware that many of the rational notions of the 1920s were in need of readjustment. They pushed for an analysis of human settlement that would go beyond the purely materialistic and functionalist approach adopted before the war. This never proved possible within CIAM itself but the foundations were certainly laid at this time for the theoretical programme that began to take shape in the wake of the large-scale concrete terrorism of the 1960s and that now also holds out the possibility of achieving better practical results.

30 Aldo van Eyck, 'De verkapte opdrachtgever en het grote woord
neen', in: *Forum* 16 (1962) no. 3, pp. 79, 80.

The history of CIAM forms a remarkable myth within the larger history of the modern movement. The problem is that although CIAM never actually led to any concrete, demonstrable result, this international movement of modern architects is usually regarded as being an immutable part of the history of modern architecture.[31] There are two arguments that may go some way towards explaining this. First of all, the modern movement is an invention of architectural historians: the architecture of our century consists of a large number of individual oeuvres that differ from one another more than the umbrella term 'modern movement' would lead one to suspect. CIAM makes it possible to draw a number of imaginary connecting lines, so that the whole structure at least has a centre of gravity. From that centre – second argument – it is possible to create a certain historical balance. The generation of H.P. Berlage, Auguste Perret and Peter Behrens forms the prehistory which is then followed by the 'Heroic Period' of legendary masterpieces of the 1920s, after which CIAM transforms this collection of fairly eccentric architecture into a practical instrument that can be used to give the enormous twentieth-century building output a recognizable 'face', which has the added advantage of making the period 1927-1959 look like a coherent chapter.

The reality is different and above all much more complex. Berlage was present at the first CIAM congress (1927), where he gave a particularly intelligent lecture about the significance of the Amsterdam School for town planning. As a thoroughly nineteenth-century architect – he was born in 1856 – he understood all too well why the Amsterdam School's street and square façades are essentially modern, but his youthful audience was so deeply contemptuous of serious architectural history that it did not want to know anything about this. CIAM never constituted a coherent whole and from its very inception there were major differences of opinion about the most basic issues. In addition, many prominent architects remained deliberately aloof from CIAM. Finally, there appears to be scarcely any continuity between the pre- and postwar years: the generation gap was just as unbridgeable in 1947 as it had been in 1927.

Like all myths, the CIAM myth is a striking example of a centuries-old dilemma, namely, the fraught relationship between reason and emotion. The pre-war CIAM was in thrall to rationalization. Every choice in the design process had to be founded on practical and scientific arguments, aesthetic arguments were regarded as emotional nonsense, worse still, as socially irresponsible frivolity. On the face of it the reasoning behind this was chiefly practical. In Germany in particular where the funds available for public housing were minimal, every form of purely outward show was regarded as extravagance. However, these constraints were also used to rationalize the search for a new architectural vocabulary: the severe modernism that in CIAM circles counted as the only true architecture, found its justification in the efforts to cut costs.

Shortly after its foundation in 1927, CIAM organized two congresses: in 1929 the theme was 'the minimum standard dwelling' while in 1930 the focus was on 'rational building methods'. The resulting publications presented a very curious picture of prevailing practical knowledge about dwellings and

31 Auke van der Woud, *Het Nieuwe Bouwen Internationaal - CIAM*, Delft 1983.

housing estates.[32] By elevating the absolute minimum to the standard, and by maintaining a highly doctrinaire interpretation of the concept of 'rational building methods', CIAM managed to imply that this was *terra incognita* for architects and town planners. In reality it was nothing of the sort. The first, and internationally very influential manual for designing modern housing estates, *Town Planning in Practice*, had been published as far back as 1909, while several first-rate housing estates had been built in Berlin during the 1920s.[33]

After 1930, under the leadership of its Dutch chairman, Van Eesteren, CIAM worked on preparations for a congress on the theme of 'the functional city'. Participants were asked to analyse a city of their choice according to specific guidelines. In order to make this at all feasible, the infinite complexity of the phenomenon of the city was reduced to four categories: dwelling, work, recreation and transportation. Van Eesteren already had some experience with such a four-function research model because it was the one used for the Algemeen Uitbreidingsplan (Amsterdam General Development Plan) on which he had worked, and which was published, together with very detailed explanatory notes, in 1934.[34] The congress, held on board of a boat sailing from Marseilles to Athens in 1933, was a resounding success and is still regarded as the high point in the history of CIAM. Nevertheless, its outcome was not at all what Van Eesteren had envisaged. He had intended it to be an introduction to the basic concepts of urbanism but the idea of the functional city proved so seductive, simple and lucid that before long it had begun to lead a life of its own.

The functional city was in fact only the last in a series of CIAM-inspired simplifications: first the minimum standard dwelling, adequate for survival but unfit for human habitation, then the housing estate, reduced to a diagrammatic development plan where all the houses had an east-west aspect, and now the city itself, reduced to the simple aggregate of four functions.

Before the war CIAM's abstract formula could not do much harm. Conservative administrators saw little point in radical innovation and tradition, in both architecture and town planning, was still very much alive. After the war, however, things were suddenly very different. A new cultural wind was blowing from the land of the victors and the general consensus was that it was time to blow the cobwebs off the old European culture once and for all. In this climate, CIAM's spartan vision of the built environment was an ideal instrument for erasing the past. By 1960 or thereabouts, the once obscure simplifications of the period around 1930 had become a standard formula for every housing programme and every urbanist intervention. The ensuing triumphant advance of the automobile would eventually end in a démasqué, for only then did the true effects of the contempt for the past underlying CIAM's vision make themselves felt. From that moment onwards people started to realize that the city was in mortal danger.

While CIAM's pre-war ideas were rapidly conquering Europe, the organization itself was being destroyed by internal differences. Young members had already started making critical noises at the first postwar gathering in 1947, but now even Le Corbusier and the first secretary, Sigfried Giedion, were hinting that a change of course was needed. Suddenly aesthetic issues were no longer taboo. The questions put by the youthful Aldo van Eyck in 1947 were especially to the point. 'The old struggle between imagina-

32 *Die Wohnung für das Existenzminimum*, Frankfurt 1930.
    Rationelle Bebauungsweisen, Frankfurt 1931.
33 Raymond Unwin, *Town Planning in Practice*, London 1909,
    reprint New York 1994.
    Norbert Huse (ed.), *Vier Berliner Siedlungen der Weimarer
    Republik*, Berlin 1987.
34 Vincent van Rossem, *Het Algemeen Uitbreidingsplan van
    Amsterdam. Geschiedenis en ontwerp*, Rotterdam 1993.

tion and common sense', he noted, 'ended tragically in favour of the latter.'[35] The rest of his discourse suggested, albeit implicitly, that CIAM's emphasis on the functional aspects of the profession was partly to blame for this. For 'the more tangible functions – those implied by the word "functionalism" – are only relevant in so far as they help to adjust man's environment more accurately to his elementary requirements. But this, after all, is no more then a necessary preliminary.'[36] The true objective was somewhat vaguely identified by Van Eyck as striving after a 'new consciousness', but he did state, rhetorically, what he thought CIAM should *not* do: 'does CIAM desire to direct the purely mechanistic improvement of the human environment or does the CIAM desire to transform this attitude, i.e. to criticize the background against which it projects its activity ?'[37]

Two years later in 1949 there was a theme-less and consequently fairly unproductive congress in Bergamo. The next gathering, held at Hoddesdon in England in 1951, was on the theme of the 'core' and this did succeed in giving the participants quite a lot to talk about. The word 'core' is a fairly general term indicating the centre of something but in the CIAM context it soon became clear that it referred to the 'heart of the city'. This opened up a dizzying perspective.

It was here that modernism to some extent dug its own theoretical grave, for any discussion of the 'heart of the city' inevitably leads to the past – to the cathedral, the market square and the town hall, to the historic centres of old cities. As a design problem the theme of the 'core' led nowhere, for the 'heart of the city' is by definition a historical datum, urbanistic, architectural, cultural and social: it is an ambience of urban life that grows by accretion, like some kind of archeological layer, in an appropriate and stable urban space. This sort of thing can never be designed; it evolves in a manner that is entirely incomprehensible to those who do not know and do not want to know the meaning of history. The theme of the 'core' introduced a vision of the city that would slowly but surely displace the idea of the functional city.

At the following congress in 1953, the youthful contingent was more outspokenly critical than ever. Their contribution to the theme of 'habitat' was human settlements in non-industrial societies. This resulted in a scathing attack on the 'sterile' nature of the functional city and its residential areas. Suddenly people could see why modern urban spaces, such as that of Roehampton Estate in London, left a disagreeable impression on Lewis Mumford and many others. Once again, history proved to be the perfect means of confronting modernism with its lack of spirituality and its emotional poverty. The historic settlement and the historic city present a very different picture; they are proof that it is possible to create an environment that can scarcely help cherishing its inhabitants.

One can, of course, dismiss this hankering for relaxed conviviality on a village square or in the wonderful urban space of an old Mediterranean city, as romantic nonsense, as an experience that is now – fatally – reserved for the annual holiday. Whether such bold cynicism is real testimony of courage is another matter. 'There is a modern form of snobbery', wrote Mitscherlich, 'which appears to be realistic and enlightened because it does not join in the sentimental dreams about the past brought on by present ills; but in fact it amounts to a shabby appeasement with everything in our present existence that is unsatisfactory, brutal, contemptible.'[38]

35 Sigfried Giedion, *A Decade of New Architecture*, Zurich 1951, p. 37.
36 Ibid.
37 Ibid.
38 Alexander Mitscherlich, *Die Unwirtlichkeit unserer Städte*, Frankfurt 1965, pp. 24, 25.

The 'habitat' theme was such a success that it was repeated, three years later, at the tenth and final congress, the organization of which was also now in the hands of the younger generation. They already began distancing themselves from the theoretical model of the functional city during the preparatory phase, shifting the emphasis instead to the problem of human relationships, to the socio-psychological factors they felt should form the basis of every architectural and urban design. The influence of the older generation was clearly waning. Van Eesteren had already been replaced as chairman shortly after the war and in 1956 Le Corbusier, too, bowed out. It looked as if there had been a complete sea change in thinking about architecture and town planning. Yet the younger CIAM generation was by no means a homogeneous group. Most of the young visitors who flocked to the last few congresses had no idea what it was all about. 'In Aix en Provence (1953)', recalled a member of the old guard, the Dutch architect W. Van Tijen, 'international architectural snobbery had discovered CIAM and people sporting sideburns, arty wives and obscure ideas clustered around Le Corbusier, basking in the reflected glory of the great man.'[39] Afterwards these groupies were never heard of again.

In the end all that remained was the group of young people known as 'Team X' who had organized the tenth congress, and a remnant of the old organization, a small committee that organized one more gathering – in the Kröller-Müller museum in Otterloo, the Netherlands, in 1959. At this meeting it became clear that the remaining young people had drawn very different and sometimes diametrically opposed conclusions from the post-war CIAM congresses. It was almost inevitable that everyone should go their own way. Of 'Team X' Aldo van Eyck later remarked succinctly that 'interests simply did not coincide'.[40] In this lecture given at the Royal Institute of British Architects in 1981, he also reiterated his opinion of the 1953 CIAM congress, recalling his futile attempts to revive the poetic spirit of the avant-garde. 'CIAM was simply not interested – the minds of its members just did not work that way. The magical appeal of technology, industrial production, systems, applied art and science (not art and science), cast a long dark shadow – clogging the mind. Floating somewhere between socialism and social welfare there was always the upward line pointing towards the future. CIAM was traumatically afraid of the wicked past.'[41]

Shortly before the final act of the CIAM drama, in September 1959, Van Eyck, together with a number of Dutch kindred spirits who included Jaap Bakema, his faithful partner in CIAM, assumed the editorship of the magazine *Forum*. The new editorial board introduced itself to readers with a handsomely illustrated issue devoted to the postwar CIAM meetings, under the title 'Het verhaal van een andere gedachte' (The Tale of a Different Idea). The message of this tale is clear. There must be an end to 'the cerebral division of urban functions and their inorganic absolutism', to 'the plethora of useless regulations and their pettyfogging enforcement', to 'the committee disease', and above all to the 'bungling of official town planning and housing authorities'.[42]

The conclusion drawn in *Forum* was fairly clear: 'we are faced with the task of creating habitable cities in a country that is even now almost uninhabitable. Genuine interiors of the community, so that each person knows who he [or she] is, so that the protective spirit can once again warm the houses, streets and squares.

39 W. van Tijen, 'In memoriam van CIAM', in: *Katholiek Bouwblad* 27 (1960) no. 3, p. 44.
40 Aldo van Eyck, 'What is and isn't Architecture. A Propos of Rats, Posts and other Pests', in: *Lotus* 28 (1981), p. 17.
41 Ibid.
42 Editorial, 'Het verhaal van een andere gedachte', in: *Forum* 14 (1959) no. 7, p. 239.

The reunion of architecture and town planning in a single discipline. A task for a more complete sort of person.'[43] There was no mention, however, of what architectural and urbanist means should be deployed in carrying out this programme.

The theoretical problems surrounding the concepts of 'core' and 'habitat' have been shrewdly analysed by the Italian art historian Carlo Argan. In a book published in 1960, *The Image of the City*, the American Kevin Lynch drew on the psychology of perception in an attempt to devise a method for designing townscapes that would be perceived as pleasant.[44] The whole book makes it painfully clear that the fundamental principle of modernism namely, that function and meaning are identical, must be regarded as wholly mistaken. In the early 1970s another American, Christopher Alexander, published two moving books in which he developed the sketchy ideas of the last CIAM gatherings into a complete theory.[45] Both Lynch and Alexander, claimed Argan, formulate an ideal that can not in fact be designed.

Both writers reject a purely rationalist vision of town planning and they do this by replacing the practical aggregate of the functional city with the concept of *ambiente*. The problem now, according to Argan, is that while space can certainly be defined with the help of a plan, *ambiente* is a conditioning phenomenon that cannot be structured or preplanned. Every historic townscape proves Lynch's point, and yet: is the development of *ambiente* something that can be programmed in advance? The same applies to an even greater degree to the approach taken by Alexander. What he refers to as the 'timeless way of building' is an autonomous process that arises from a completely natural relationship between man and his environment. This implies that it would be better to do away with town planning altogether.[46]

The fact is that urbanism is indissolubly connected with the organization and design of the urban space, and this is achieved by means of a plan. In Argan's view, the radical functionalists' mistake was to think that it was necessary and feasible to change the urban space in a revolutionary manner. It is not the urbanist's task to create a new world but rather, within the constraints imposed by the existing order and using the means at his disposal, to steer urban life in the right direction.[47] The city is a historical given, that is to say the product of both continuity and permanent change. This is why it behoves town planners to be cautious and conservative, by nature reforming, striving always for a harmonious balance between the historic city and necessary change. The notion of a perfectly functioning city is as mistaken as the notion of a city representing a timeless order. In the last instance, historical thinking is more fruitful than utopian longing, whether it is projected into the future or the past.

43 Ibid.
44 Kevin Lynch, *The Image of the City*, Cambridge Mass. 1960.
45 Christopher Alexander, *The Timeless Way of Building*, New York 1979.
   Christopher Alexander, *A Pattern Language*, New York 1977.
46 Giulio Carlo Argan, *Kunstgeschichte als Stadtgeschichte*, Munich 1989 (Rome 1984), pp. 262, 263.
47 Op. cit. p. 265.

For centuries historical thought has formed the backbone of architectural consciousness. The Greeks borrowed their models from Egyptian architecture, the Romans copied the art in turn from the Greeks. After lying dormant for a thousand years, the classical vocabulary was the subject of intensive historical and theoretical study during the Renaissance in Italy. Since then architecture has continued to elaborate on these themes, producing many variations of neo-classicism down the centuries. Even in the nineteenth century when new methods of construction and new materials started to appear in rapid succession, no one saw any need to force a radical break with the past. Indeed, even at the beginning of the present century the classical tradition was still immensely influential. Peter Behrens, Adolf Loos and Auguste Perret, the founding fathers of twentieth-century architecture, designed modern rather than modernist buildings.

The modernists' vilification of architecture as a historical phenomenon, which has never been satisfactorily analysed, was frighteningly successful. In a surprisingly short time all essential knowledge of architecture was erased from both architectural training and design practice – seldom has an intellectual discipline been so effectively trivialized – and what remained was construction, standard floor plans and a few pointless Le Corbusier quotations. Only one country managed miraculously to escape this wholesale purge of the past: Italy. This was in no small measure due to the Milanese architect Ernesto Rogers, although Giuseppe Samonà and Bruno Zevi among others also did their bit. Whereas the rest of Europe only discovered the significance of the historic city at a much later date, in Italy it was a matter of serious discussion right after the war.[48]

What we now see as the almost laughable arrogance – or folly – with which architects elsewhere in Europe ignored the urban context of their buildings, was unthinkable in Italy where it was virtually impossible to close one's eyes to architectural history in line with modernist dogma. This was true not only in cities like Rome and Venice, where the presence of the past can sometimes be almost oppressive, but also, perhaps especially, in Milan, the most modern city in Italy. Here of all places, a nineteenth-century industrial city so scarred by inept town planning policies and war damage that it scarcely resembled an ancient Italian city, there was good reason to ponder whether radical modernism was necessarily synonymous with progress. Some Italian architects had in fact been doing this before the war, witness the string of very striking buildings produced between 1920 and 1940 by the Novecento Movement centred around Giovanni Muzio and Adolf Loos's pupil, Giuseppe de Finetti.[49] Although stylistically this architecture is quite different from that of the Amsterdam School, there are typological affinities in that both architectural movements respected the urban block as a fundamental urban element. Nor is it any accident that the first historical examination of this Dutch approach to the urban block in the period 1920-1940 should have been written by a Milanese architect.[50]

The Italians' efforts to escape the rigor mortis of prevailing architectural thought did not win them any friends elsewhere in Europe. In 1959 Reyner Banham published a stern admonitory article in *The Architectural Review*, under the heading: 'The Italian Retreat from Modern Architecture'.[51] In fact, as Tafuri

48 Manfredo Tafuri, *History of Italian Architecture 1944-1985*, Cambridge Mass. 1989 (Turin 1982), p. 6.

49 Annegret Burg, *Stadtarchitektur Mailand 1920-1940*, Basle 1992 (Milan 1991).

50 G. Canella, 'L'epopea borghese della Scuola di Amsterdam', in: *Casabella* 1957 no. 215, pp. 76-91.

51 Reyner Banham, 'Neoliberty - The Italian Retreat from Modern Architecture', in: *The Architectural Review*, 1959 no. 747, pp. 281-285.

remarked, the article focused on a fairly harmless triviality rather than the essence of the Italian deviation, but the English critic's irritation and the rhetorical nature of his argument are typical of the stubborn persistence with which many people clung to the modernist creed.[52] His criticism was directed at a building in Turin by Roberto Gabetti and Aimaro Isola that displayed *Jugendstil* stylistic characteristics. In addition, Banham not only detected references in recent Italian work to Otto Wagner, Charles Rennie Mackintosh and the Amsterdam School, but also suspected that there was an unhealthy interest in brick south of the Alps.

'There is a widespread feeling', wrote Banham, 'that much that was of value in the architecture and theory current before 1914 was lost or buried in overhasty stylistic formulations in the early Twenties, and then forgotten during the Academic phase of the Thirties... .'[53] In his view this was a totally mistaken analysis, or rather, he regarded the whole issue as an irrelevance. For, so the argument went, 'events have moved too fast, even in the Forties, for there to be any time for architecture to go back and re-puzzle its earlier problems.'[54] This embargo on any reflection whatsoever during the process of designing is one of the implicit but very typical dogmas of modernism. Questioning and attempting to arrive at an independent opinion by way of critical reflection were old-fashioned activities that an 'irreversible revolution' had long since tossed on the rubbish dump of history.

Banham cited as important items of this 'cultural revolution' the vacuum cleaner, the electric cooker, the gramophone and other appliances that were supposed to have radically changed the nature of domestic life and even the 'meaning of domestic architecture'. In this context Futurism, the influence of Frank Lloyd Wright, Adolf Loos, the German architect Hermann Muthesius and Cubism had also to be seen as elements of a cultural watershed. While this may perhaps be true of Futurism, Wright, Loos and Muthesius built houses that can be lived in in a very old-fashioned, conventional and comfortable manner – in spite of the vacuum cleaner. Picasso never exhibited the slightest interest or sympathy for the superficialities of modern life – his work was utterly painterly – and he preferred to live in old country houses. Banham's arguments are no more than an expression of faith, and it was on this basis that he categorized the developments in Milan and Turin as 'infantile regression'.

This neither particularly subtle nor very elegant critique of Italian endeavours was repeated loud and clear during the final gathering of CIAM members in Otterloo in 1959, where Giancarlo de Carlo, Ignazio Gardella and Ernesto Rogers faced a barrage of ungracious criticism of their work.[55] During the discussion with Rogers about his Torre Velasca in Milan, Jaap Bakema said: 'you are resisting contemporary life'.[56] The fact that this many-storeyed building was less than five hundred metres from the cathedral seemed to have escaped Bakema's attention, as had the fact that Gardella's apartment block in Venice merged very subtly with a vulnerable historic townscape. As the Dutch architectural historian Ed Taverne has rightly concluded, it was from this moment that Dutch architecture became trapped in a provincial backwater.[57]

Roberto Gabetti en Aimaro Isola, Bottega d'Erasmo, Turijn, 1953

52 Tafuri 1989 (see note 48), pp. 54, 55.
53 Banham 1959 (see note 51), p. 285.
54 Ibid.
55 Tafuri 1989 (see note 48), p. 58.
56 Ed Taverne, 'Towards an open aesthetic - Ambities in de Nederlandse architectuur 1948-1959', in: Bernard Leupen (ed.), *Hoe modern is de Nederlandse architectuur?*, Rotterdam 1990, p. 54.
57 Op. cit. p. 47.

Bakema's appointment as professor of architecture in Delft in 1963 meant that there, too, architectural training was reduced to a level that can only be described as fatuous.

While the bizarre debate between traditionalists and modernists at Delft started to look more and more like an empty farce, Italian architectural training developed a remarkable synthesis between architectural design and historical thought, an educational programme perfectly encapsulated by the Torre Velasca. It was, claimed Tafuri, '(...) symptomatic of the Milanese climate of the late 1950s'.[58] Its multiplicity of functions makes it an essential part of the urban fabric, albeit vertically organized, while stylistically it is a synthesis of traditional regional architecture and the urbane classicism of Perret. With this design Rogers demonstrated that it was possible to make a building using only urbanist and architectural means, without invoking the tired rhetoric of modernism and without CIAM's moralistic self-justification.

It was Aldo Rossi, a student of Rogers, who provided his teacher's work with a theoretical foundation. His book, *The Architecture of the City* is, as Peter Eisenman writes in the foreword to the American edition, an attempt to redefine the position and role of the architect.[59] Just as Rossi had lost interest in Banham's revolutionary rhetoric, so his generation had come to regard the idealistic pretensions of architecture as so many hollow phrases.[60] Rossi asked himself what (leaving the vacuum cleaners and ambitious socialist aldermen aside for a moment) architecture really amounted to.

His answer came in the form of the aforementioned book which appeared in Italian in 1966, but was not published in English until 1982, whereas the German translation had already appeared in 1973. *The Architecture of the City* is a curious book – students who have had to read it for an exam always claim that it makes for fascinating reading but they are incapable of giving a clear account of its contents. Rossi's prose, writes Tafuri, is tautological: the city is architecture and architecture is the city.[61] On occasion, however, it can be reasonably clear: 'when a project or a form is not utopian or abstract but evolves from the specific problems of the city, it persists and expresses these problems both through its style and form, as well as through its many deformations.'[62] Sometimes it is clearer still: 'I think that architecture only exists when architects plainly refer to historical processes manifest in the urban continuity.'[63]

Rossi advocates an architecture that is by definition part of a greater whole, not just physically, as part of the urban fabric, but also theoretically, as a reflection of

58 Tafuri 1989 (see note 48), p. 51.
59 Aldo Rossi, *The Architecture of the City*, Cambridge Mass. 1982 (Padua 1966), p. 5.
60 David Watkin, *Morality and Architecture*, Oxford 1977.
61 Tafuri 1989 (see note 488), p. 141.
62 Rossi 1982 (see note 59), p. 18.
63 S. Umberto Barbieri, 'Een stad en een architect - een gesprek over Venetië met Aldo Rossi', in: *Wonen TABK* 1985 no. 18, p. 31.

top: Ernesto Rogers et al, Torre Velasca, Milan, 1950-1951, construction completed in 1958
bottom: Ignazio Gardella, Apartment Building, Zattere, Venice, 1954-58

architectural history. The tautological nature of his argument stems from the fact that the city is a cryptogram and behind every architectural idea lies another architectural idea. The labyrinthine character of *The Architecture of the City* is a direct consequence of its unwillingness to answer the question of what architecture is. In a certain sense the building lines are more important than the appearance of the buildings, yet it is the buildings that confer permanence on the building lines. The question of what architecture is cannot be answered with a stylistic formula and a discourse on functions; it is a permanent interplay between building and city which, if properly understood, results in architecture.

Although *The Architecture of the City* is essentially about anonymous architecture, Rossi is definitely interested in the contributions of individual architects. In the late 1950s the work of Adolf Loos was a major source of inspiration, while his interest in H.P. Berlage ultimately led to an exhibition in Venice of the Dutch architect's multi-faceted oeuvre – 'a great eclecticist' according to Rossi. In 1973 he curated an exhibition in Milan entitled *Rational Architecture*, which was the first survey of important work realized after the demise of the modern movement. It must have been a fascinating event; three members of the 'New York Five' (Peter Eisenman, Michael Graves and John Hejduk) put in an appearance as did the brothers Leon and Rob Krier, Mathias Ungers, Carlo Aymonino and Adolfo Natalini. It was not long before people were talking about 'La Tendenza', a new architectural tendency. Tafuri argued that they did not form a coherent group, but now, over twenty years after the event, it is possible to conclude that this kaleidoscope of individual talent did in fact provide a fairly accurate picture of the future.[64]

64 Tafuri 1989 (see note 48), p. 142.

Palladio as benchmark: Colin Rowe

The contribution to the postwar architectural debate of the English-American Colin Rowe, teacher of the 'New York Five', was initially rather obscure, but since he was awarded the English Royal Gold Medal for architecture in 1995 there can be no longer be any doubt about the influential nature of his publications. Rowe made his début in 1947 with an essay, 'The Mathematics of the Ideal Villa', that appeared in *The Architectural Review*.[65] This analysis of Le Corbusier's Villa Stein demonstrated that it is possible to regard the masterpieces of the modern movement as pure architecture, that is, without the ideological veneer of cultural revolution and the like. Rowe had learnt from Rudolf Wittkower, an architectural historian, the precise nature of the relationship between Andrea Palladio and the English eighteenth-century country house.[66] Applying this analytical method to the Villa Stein he came to the remarkable conclusion that it had been modelled on Palladio's Villa Foscari (Villa Malcontenta 1550-1560).

The story goes that Wittkower was not best pleased by the way his pupil had linked Palladio to modern architecture, but for many people the article was a breath of fresh air. 'Rowe's scholarly iconoclasm', Banham recalled later, 'his appeal to purely architectural explanations of modern architecture, rather then socio-functional Zeitgeistlichkeit, were almost irresistible'.[67] Unfortunately the output of this discerning critic was slender and it was not until 1976 that a collection of his essays appeared in print.[68] This volume can be regarded as the first serious attack on the mythology of the modern movement. Simply by looking carefully and trusting to his common sense, Rowe was able, time and time again, to show that many of the fine words expended on architecture belong to the category of idle gossip. It is an invigorating read, almost as if Rowe's pen were renovating the buildings he describes, stripping them of all the sticky glue applied by writers like Nikolaus Pevsner, Sigfried Giedion and Leonardo Benevolo in their efforts to cement them into a canonical history.[69]

Rowe's attitude to the modern movement has always been critical, rather ironic at first, in his early essays, later scathing, and in his most recent book somewhat milder again but also more aloof. After a series of articles about architecture in 1975 he published a lengthy essay on modern urban development in *The Architectural Review*, entitled 'Collage City'.[70] It was obvious that Rowe had been influenced by Rossi's book about the relationship between architecture and the city, but 'Collage City' was more contentious and directed more towards urbanist practice. Le Corbusier's utopian and highly schematic vision of the modern city came in for particularly sharp criticism. Rowe was probably the first to illustrate the literal collapse of this urban design ideal – Mumford's reviled high-rise in an amorphous space – with the now-famous photograph of the dynamiting of the Pruitt-Igoe housing estate in St. Louis in 1972.

65 Colin Rowe, 'The Mathematics of the Ideal Villa', in: *The Mathematics of the Ideal Villa and Other Essays*, Cambridge Mass. 1976.

66 Rudolf Wittkower, *Palladio and English Palladianism*, London 1974.

67 Reyner Banham, 'A Fifth Column for Corbu', in: *The Times Literary Supplement*, 76 (1977) no. 3914 (18 March).

68 Rowe 1976 (see note 65); Colin Rowe, *As I was saying. Recollections and Miscellaneous Essays*, Cambridge Mass. 1996.

69 Nikolaus Pevsner, *Pioneers of Modern Design*, London 1936; Sigfried Giedion, *Space, Time and Architecture*, Cambridge Mass. 1941; Leonardo Benevolo, *History of Modern Architecture*, Cambridge Mass. 1977 (Bari 1960).
Only Henry-Russel Hitchcock presented a markedly different view of the history of modern architecture: *Architecture. Nineteenth & Twentieth Centuries*, London 1958, see: Rowe 1996

top: *Andrea Palladio, Villa Foscari, Malcontenta, 1559-1560*

top right: *Le Corbusier, Plan of the Centre of Saint Dié, 1945*

bottom right: *Plan of the Centre of Parma, XXX Century*

(see note 68), Vol. 1, pp. 177-184.

70 Colin Rowe, 'Collage City', in: *The Architectural Review* 158 (1975) no. 942. Published in book form by MIT Press, Cambridge Mass. 1979. See also: Colin Rowe, 'The Present Urban Predicament', in: *American Architectural Quarterly*, 11 (1979) no. 4, pp. 40-48.

Rowe drew the radical conclusion that a building that has no relation to the spatial structure of the city loses all its significance. The meaning of 'urban spatial structure' was clearly spelt out by a juxtaposition of two illustrations in the more detailed version of the article that appeared in book form. The reader sees a design by Le Corbusier that was presented to members of the eighth CIAM congress in 1951 as a representation of the 'core' (the centre of St. Dié), alongside the street map of the old town centre of Parma. 'The matrix of the city', commented Rowe, 'has become transformed from continuous solid to continuous void.'[71] This, as subsequent history has made painfully clear, was a fundamental error. The traditional concept of urban space, with street and square walls, alleyways and courtyards, is crucial to the city dweller's perception of city life.

This insight had been fairly dramatic for Rossi because he was confronted with the question of how an architect who no longer believed in progress could actually continue to think. Rowe, as a historian, saw no such methodological problem. As even observant tourists understand, every city is a collage of urban fragments, and this arrangement has resulted in an almost infinite richness of urban space. If the radical alternative has so clearly failed then it surely makes sense to return to the unwritten laws of historical urban development. Rowe illustrated this suggestion with a brief but highly imaginative 'excursion' into the history of the city. It is significant that it was in his criticism of the modern movement's approach to town planning in particular that Rowe reached such a decidedly negative verdict.

In his most recent book, *The Architecture of Good Intentions*, where town planning is conspicuous by its absence, Rowe is more generously disposed. The tone is not only mild but also detached: in the twenty years that have passed since the publication of 'Collage City' modernism has gradually lost all significance for the current architectural debate. The modern movement has now finally become a historical issue, as Rowe indicates in his subtitle: 'towards a possible retrospect'. The word 'possible' underlines the fact that the book does not pretend to pass final judgement – it is indeed more in the nature of a reconnaissance, a look back in

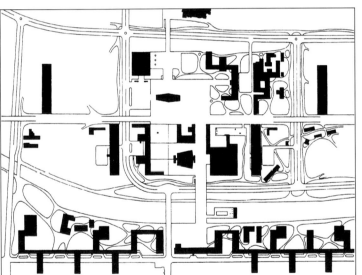

amazement. But one thing is at any rate clear: 'For rather more than forty years it has been apparent that the Architecture of good intentions has been no unmitigated blessing; and, therefore, quite simply it cannot be presented, or justified, via the agency of any innocent story with a happy ending. (...) No. The presentation of modern architecture as the heroine of an unproblematic Victorian novel has, to say the least, evidently become too absurd.'[72]

For those readers who have not yet grasped this point, Rowe confesses in a postscript to being a 'highly sceptical devotee of modern architecture'. Before this he has dealt with five themes: epistemology, eschatology, iconography, mechanism and organicism. In each case he demonstrates that the theoretical foundations of the modern movement are a strange concoction of mainly half-baked nineteenth-century theories,

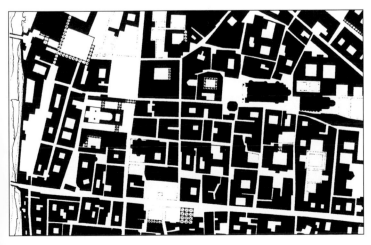

71 Colin Rowe, *Collage City*, Cambridge Mass. 1979, p. 56.
72 Colin Rowe, *The Architecture of Good Intentions*, London 1994, p. 13.

yet oddly enough this scarcely detracts from the charm of the works displayed. On page 130 Rowe shows two houses by the nineteenth-century Dutch innovator P.J.H. Cuypers alongside Gerrit Rietveld's Schröder House. Lop a bit off the top of Cuypers's houses in your mind's eye, he suggests, remove a few details and paint them white and the result bears a close resemblance to the Schröder House. In other words, is it really true that Cubism had such a tremendous impact on 1920s' architecture?

The first two chapters are the most critical, perhaps partly because in these Rowe did not allow himself to be diverted by the charm of architectural masterpieces which the enthusiast in him simply cannot resist. In the first chapter, on epistemology, he condemns the indiscriminate use of the term 'modern'. It was in fact a strange formulation that linked technology and function to a typically nineteenth-century notion, namely that of the 'spirit of the age'. No one noticed the internal contradiction, for the formulation was in fact extremely superficial. 'Professing to be logical, the architect did not choose to examine such purely logical problems. For his consciousness was inflamed by a far more urgent business. Like St. Paul on his way to Damascus he had become the victim of a revelation.'[73]

Architectural theory had become increasingly moralistic in tone during the nineteenth century.[74] The traditional problems of decorum, good taste and so on, gradually gave way to a genuine eschatological vision in which only architecture could save the world from ruin. In the early nineteenth century the English theorist A.W.N. Pugin advocated a revival of Gothic architecture, not because it was more beautiful but because only this Christian architecture could save the world from the clutches of the industrial monster. Though the form and content of this argument differed, the one constant was a tremendous overestimation of the social significance of architecture. Architecture can give expression, and even lend a certain dignity, to social life, but it is absurd to think that social life might be determined by the built environment.

During the 1920s a number of architects became firmly convinced that only modern architecture and modern urbanism could prevent the industrial world from descending into total chaos. In the last instance it was this 'revelation' that gave the architecture of the modern movement its dogmatic character. 'It can scarcely be exaggeration', wrote Rowe, 'to propose that the modern movement typically conceived of itself in the form of a church – a church which had its eschatology and its millennial hopes, its full complement of prophets, martyrs, apostles; a church which made it possible to use a building in much the same way that a devout member of the Greek Church may use an icon – because the icon exists, primarily, not for the sake of aesthetic contemplation; it exists for excitation of religious sentiment. Its aesthetic virtues are secondary, and something comparable was certainly the case in the example of modern architecture. The modern building may have satisfied physical requirements; it may have possessed virtue; but, fundamentally, it existed because of cultural fantasies. That is: for the most part it was an elaborate icon. It was an icon of change, an icon of technology, an icon of the good society, an icon of the future. Presented for the adoration of the faithful (whose numbers rapidly increased), it was a magical therapeutic image.'[75] So long as this involves no more than the odd villa or two it is not a problem, but when hundreds of thousands of people have to live in buildings and on housing estates designed as iconographic ideals it can, as experience has shown, lead to a lot of unnecessary misery.

73 Op. cit. p. 29.
74 Watkin 1977 (see note 60).
75 Rowe 1994 (see note 72), p. 42.

The scathing tone adopted by Rowe in 'Collage City' was to some extent typical of the 1970s. During the 1950s there was still cause for doubt; it looked as if the modern movement was not yet past redemption. During the 1960s, however, it became clear that modernism had become a destructive force, a disaster that in many European cities had wreaked more havoc than the war. Continual increases in scale in the building industry resulted in a kind of building type, in both housing and office building, that no longer had anything at all to do with architecture. Especially in the Netherlands, with its strong tradition of puritanical tight-fistedness, the concrete climbed skywards in all its glorious anonymity. At the same time town planners attempted with unprecedented destructiveness to clear a path for the car.

It is no wonder that after this disastrous decade many people turned their backs on the modernists' collapsed house of cards. In fact, Rossi's 1973 exhibition in Milan was a bit premature. Not long afterwards there were signs of a change of heart in the work of Michael Graves, while the work of Adolfo Natalini also changed character in the course of the 1970s. Very cautiously, it seems, people once again dared to look further back into history, beyond the fault lines of the 1920s. As we shall see, this was no easy task. In the day-to-day practice of both design and building much traditional know-how had been lost. Nobody looking at a pre-war textbook 'for the builder and bricklayer' can fail to be struck by the fact that the original profusion of architectural means of expression has been reduced to a pathetic minimum in the present-day building industry.

Yet because of the modern movement's systematic smear campaign against anything that did not embrace the principles of the avant-garde, the concept of tradition has also been discredited. It is conveniently assumed that tradition can never be anything other that a dusty museum, where change is by definition impossible. This, however, is rhetorical nonsense for it also implies that architects like Filippo Brunelleschi, Leon Battista Alberti and all the other masters of the classical tradition did not play a vital role in the development of architecture. Yet recent architectural historical research has shown that there was never any question of slavish imitation, quite the contrary: experiment and innovation were the order of the day within the framework of the classical tradition.[76] The notion that a traditional framework can never be anything but conservative rests on a wholly one-sided, if not simplistic notion of historical development.

In his notes for the 'Rational Architecture' exhibition, Rossi found himself obliged to state clearly once again that the study of the past did not automatically lead to the construction of copies. 'We remain insensitive to all accusations of historicism: we have simply removed from schools the boring courses of historic enumeration, in order to repropose a history of architecture as a living part of architecture. History must be seen from the point of view of today's struggles, rather than as an enumeration of events.'[77] When it comes to the relationship between architecture and the city, Rossi explained a few lines further on, one cannot avoid certain fundamental principles: '(...) typological forms that offer that set of conditions which are not architectural phantasies, but upon which the architect only intervenes to perfect and pursue in today's terms.'[78]

76 Liane Lefaivre, 'Rethinking the Western Humanist
Tradition', in: *Design Book Review*, 1994 no. 34, pp. 1-3.
77 Aldo Rossi, 'Rational Architecture', in: Aldo Rossi, *Selected
Writings and Projects*, London 1983, p. 56.
78 Op. cit. p. 57.

In Milan Rossi also exhibited the plans Rob Krier had made with students for the reconstruction of the centre of Stuttgart, blighted by acts of war and traffic corridors. This same work, prefaced by two introductory chapters about the theory of the urban space, was published by Krier in 1975 in the book *Stadtraum* (Urban Space).[79] In the early 1970s urbanist thinking in Europe was little more than an arithmetical model. The urban development plan no longer existed: planners calculated the proper number of square metres of housing and municipal green space after which contractors, scarcely hampered by architects, could go ahead and build their gallery-access flats.

It was high time, Rob Krier argued, to draw the unavoidable conclusion from this sorry state of affairs that the experiment of modern urbanism had largely failed. After fifty years of intellectual demolition work in the profession, all knowledge of the urban structure as a synthesis of architecture, urban space and social intercourse had vanished. As such it was necessary to return to a very elementary level of thought, to questions such as: how does a square work, and what makes a street a street? The age-old art of creating the urban space had to be more or less reinvented.

In *Stadtraum* Krier gives a brief but richly illustrated introduction to the typology and morphology of urban space. The drawings reflect the enormous variation that is so characteristic of the streets and squares of historic cities; the explanatory text is clearly written, hence also intelligible to ordinary citizens, and is often even pointed. The basic premise is simple; Krier is convinced '(...) that in our modern cities we have lost sight of the traditional understanding of urban space.'[80] It is difficult to give a really convincing historical explanation for this. The pre-war modernists were interested only in the disadvantages of the perimeter block, regarding open development as ideal. Reality, of course, is a lot more complicated; in a genuine urban context the perimeter block probably has more advantages than disadvantages but an unbiased comparison has never been made. The modernists were obsessed by light and air, and in their eyes it was absolutely necessary, with a view to the sunlighting, that all dwellings be oriented in the selfsame – east-west – direction. This was a very one-sided approach and sure enough it had fatal repercussions for traditional town planning. 'Our age', Krier concludes, 'has a remarkably distorted sense of history, which can only be characterised as irrational.'[81]

The modern city of course functions differently from, say, a medieval city, and Krier is not blind to this fact. On the market square the social function of the café has generally superseded that of churchgoing; in the past, social life was played out much more on the street than in the living room but TV and video have changed all that. In addition, of course, motor traffic has had a devastating effect on the livability of public space. If we really want to save something of public life in our cities – and we should not underestimate the importance of this for social life in general – then we have no alternative but to create wherever possible spaces that are pleasant to be in.

This entails a number of conditions. First of all the obtrusive presence of the car makes the urban space inhospitable to humans. Then there are a number of aesthetic requirements that must be met. The size, scale and proportions must be such that human beings, who are after all of a specific size and who move in a specific way, experience a sense of harmony with the built environment. It is fairly obvious that those cities

79 Rob Krier, *Stadtraum in Theorie und Praxis*, Stuttgart 1975.
80 Op. cit. p. 1.
81 Op. cit. p. 2.

that were once built with the radius of action and perceptions of the pedestrian in mind, are an ideal training ground for this type of urbanist thinking. Examples are scattered throughout Europe and there is little or no dispute about the quality of the historic city as a place to stay. The presence of so many tourists speaks for itself.

Krier has assembled an instructive survey of what old European cities have to offer when it comes to congenial urban space, but this in itself does not solve the problem. A host of factors make it well nigh impossible to work with such urbanist concepts nowadays. Contemporary building practice is wholly geared to enabling the city dweller to function as a motorist. People have become accustomed to entering buildings not via a street entrance, let alone a square, but via an underground car park. The gallery-access flat has also robbed the streetscape of front doors; the ground floor consists entirely of storage areas. Local governments carpet the public area with asphalt, or at best (as in the case along the canals in Amsterdam) with concrete bricks and concrete kerbing. Even in the provision of something as basic as good and attractive paving the day-to-day practice is woefully inadequate.

'The need to meet the town's function of poetry of space', according to Krier, 'should be as self-evident as the need to meet any technical requirements. In a purely objective sense, it is just as basic.'[82] This proposition has far-reaching consequences. Office and housing blocks must start to function differently, the authorities must stop relegating streets and squares to the bottom of an already tight budget, and above all architects must learn to consider their design as part of a larger whole. Implicit in this last, as Rob Krier is also aware, is a fundamental criticism of the prevailing architectural culture. Beside a series of sketches of potential urban spaces he remarks: 'I would like to try and convince architectural theoreticians and historians that in the future they must incorporate spatial considerations more exactly into their overall view of architecture and town planning. Such considerations have in fact been criminally neglected.'[83]

Stadtraum closes with an afterword aimed at architects where Krier enlarges on the architectural critique touched on above. The main point of this critique is eloquently illustrated by two drawings showing the effect of modern urbanism on the urban structure. In the left-hand drawing we see a coherent whole of streets and squares and the development consists of perimeter blocks. The right-hand drawing depicts the

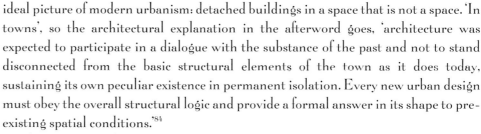

ideal picture of modern urbanism: detached buildings in a space that is not a space. 'In towns', so the architectural explanation in the afterword goes, 'architecture was expected to participate in a dialogue with the substance of the past and not to stand disconnected from the basic structural elements of the town as it does today, sustaining its own peculiar existence in permanent isolation. Every new urban design must obey the overall structural logic and provide a formal answer in its shape to pre-existing spatial conditions.'[84]

This may seem obvious, even simple, but the problem is that contemporary architectural designs by definition ignore their surroundings. This is because modern architecture is designed according to a method that works from the inside out. Working from the brief, the architect proceeds systematically, it must be admitted, to

82 Op. cit. p. 6.
83 Op. cit. p. 16.
84 Op. cit. p. 149.

Rob Krier and Students, Reconstruction of the Centre of Stuttgart (Österreichischer Platz), 1973

develop a plan, then the structure and finally a few minor details such as access, technical services and ducts. The final appearance is merely the end result of a kind of meter-cupboard logic. Hence there is no roof because the technical services now stand in a sort of container on the spot where the roof used to be. There is no rear elevation because that is where the galleries are suspended, nor is there a front elevation, for the terrorism of the plan allows no scope at all for turning this façade into an architectural composition that harmonizes with the surrounding buildings.

In the light of the above it is understandable that Krier should close with a radical but not very optimistic postscript. He dares to raise the question of the compulsive innovation dominating current design practice but does so in the knowledge that he will be misunderstood. 'I would go so far as to maintain that nowadays it is more useful to imitate something "old" but proven, rather than to turn out something new which risks causing people suffering. The logical and attractive building types and spatial structures left to us by anonymous architects have been improved upon by countless succeeding generations. They have matured into masterpieces even in the absence of a single creator of genius, because they were based on a perfectly refined awareness of building requirements using simple means; the result of an accurate understanding of tradition as the vehicle for passing on technical and artistic knowledge. All my dire warnings inspire considerable gloom, and one fears that it will prove impossible to do justice to the demands I have outlined.'[85]

Nonetheless, *Stadtraum* was reasonably successful; it was read in professional circles and the English translation has been through five reprints. Krier's thesis that modern urbanism is bankrupt has been accepted in general terms but his alternative, the suggestion to inject new life into traditional urbanism, has had few tangible results. Even in his own professional practice Krier has seldom been given the opportunity to give concrete expression to his vision of the city. In the postscript to a recent book about his work, published in 1993, he writes as follows: 'This book can unfortunately only hint at what I would like to have

achieved in practice, during my 30-year struggle for a valid conception of urban development structures and integrated clear housing typologies. For many years, vehement criticism of my work and defamatory public disputes consumed an excessive amount of my energy and time. When I did get a chance to build, the modest budgets (for the social housing for example), along with the undermining of the architect's authority in the construction process, ensured that my ideal concepts were realised only in schematic form.

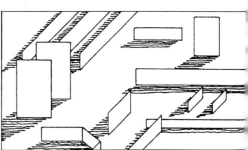

I still find it miraculous that I had a chance to build two real squares: the Schinkelplatz in Berlin and the Camillo-Sitte Platz in Vienna. 20 years ago, when I was working on the Urban Space book, I would never have believed that I would be so lucky. Though these places are modest in scope, I know that they will provide a fitting setting for public life, blossoming with time and growing old gracefully. No architecture critic's commentary could give me an equal sense of success. My very traditional approach to architecture and urbanism sets me – and a few friends – far

85 Op. cit. p. 150.

apart from successful mainstream architecture at the end of this millennium.'[86]

Some elements of this litany are of course part and parcel of the standard tragedy of the architectural profession: too few commissions, too tight a budget, a contractor who knows better, and so on. However, two points, which together form the crux of the matter, are of genuine concern. First of all Krier restates here very clearly that his work presupposes a unity between architecture and city, between building and urbanism. His designs can only be realized if the development slots typologically into the form of the public space as defined in the urban design plan. This presupposes a decidedly unfashionable design method. Krier speaks of his 'very traditional approach' to architectural design. These two points, the compelling connection between structure and urban space, and the accompanying emphasis on the importance of tradition, make the realization of Krier's urbanist work problematical. Since the unprecedented success of the Centre Pompidou, architects are no longer interested in tradition, and for many critics the idea of tradition is still plainly suspect, hence the harsh criticism Krier complains of.

Krier has explained his traditional approach to the profession further in a detailed book entitled *Architectural Composition*.[87] Any architect who works on an urban plan designed by Krier would do well to make a thorough study of this book and of course, *Stadtraum*. But designers who have been nurtured on the logic of the meter cupboard cannot magically be retrained by a single book on architectural form. Moreover, neither *Architectural Composition* nor *Stadtraum* satisfactorily explains just what is meant by the integration of dwelling typologies and the urban plan – and this in particular is a fundamental issue. The architectural historian thinks almost automatically of the famous words of a German colleague enthusiastically cited by Berlage in 1909: 'Städte bauen heißt mit dem Hausmaterial Raum gestalten (building cities means creating space with housing.).'[88] Today's architects have not the slightest idea how to go about it.

86 Rob Krier, *Architecture and Urban Design*, London 1993, p. 44.
87 Rob Krier, *Architectural Composition*, London 1988; appeared in Stuttgart in 1989 as *Ueber architektonische Komposition*.
88 A.E. Brinckmann, *Platz und Monument. Untersuchungen zur Geschichte und Aesthetik der Stadtbaukunst in neuerer Zeit*, Berlin 1908, p. 170. Cited approvingly by H.P. Berlage, 'Het Uitbreidingsplan van 's-Gravenhage', in: *Bouwkunst*, 1 (1909) no. 4/5, p. 97.

left: Rob Krier, traditional and modernistic urban space
top and bottom right: Rob Krier, Camillo-Sitte Platz, Vienna,
1981-1987; top: plans and elevations

It is useful to look at the formula 'Städte bauen heißt met dem Hausmaterial Raum gestalten' and its concrete application in Berlin and Amsterdam in more detail, partly because this also provides an opportunity to place the criticism directed at Krier in a historical framework. In this criticism – as is perhaps always the case – it is possible to distinguish three tones of voice: sympathetic incomprehension, irritable incomprehension, and downright hostility.

An example of sympathetic incomprehension is to be found, oddly enough, in Colin Rowe's foreword to the English translation of *Stadtraum*. Although Rowe, given his own position, can sympathize with Krier's ambition to awaken interest in tradition in urban development, he feels that Krier is formulating an extreme standpoint in *Stadtraum*. It is, according to Rowe, '(...) eminently conservative in its tone'.[89] Krier's criticism of modern urbanism is indeed radical but it does not follow that he takes a conservative position. This misunderstanding is typical of the twentieth-century architectural debate conducted according to the stereotypical thinking of the modern movement: he who is not with us is against us and hence against progress. The possibility that there might be another, genuinely 'modern' twentieth-century architecture is simply excluded. This, of course, is nonsense; the Delft School, to mention a Dutch example, belongs unmistakably to the architecture of this century. The critics of the modern movement are not suggesting that sewerage, electricity and piped water should be abolished; it is rather a matter of aesthetic disagreements, in which context one can hardly speak of progress.

Rowe is, as he himself writes, a 'highly sceptical believer' when it comes to modern architecture. In the last instance the modern movement remains for him the all-embracing framework within which tradition functions as an intellectual game of references and erudition that is not entirely free of a certain snobbery. Krier, on the other hand, is convinced that tradition – urbanist and hence also architectural – should be normative. Rowe regards this as an almost incomprehensible alternative: 'that Rob Krier somehow doesn't fit, that he cannot rapidly be relegated to a category, might quite well be the first observation.'[90] For such an experienced critic this is a remarkably hesitant judgement. It so happens that Rob Krier fits perfectly into a category that played a major role in the history of architecture and town planning up to the 1920s. In 1992 Vittorio Lampugnani arranged an impressive exhibition on this category of modern but not modernist architects in the Deutsches Architekturmuseum in Frankfurt under the telling title, 'Reform and Tradition'.[91] And earlier still, in 1979, the German architectural historian Julius Posener published a detailed study of the cautious modernization of German architecture in the period 1885-1914, and this book, too, shows that tradition and modernization can coexist harmoniously.

Even in his sympathetic conclusion, the picture Rowe gives of *Stadt-*

89 Krier 1979 (see note 79), p. 10.
90 Ibid.
91 Vittorio Lampugnani, Romana Schneider, *Moderne Architektur in Deutschland 1900 bis 1950. Reform und Tradition*, Stuttgart 1992.

top: *Ludwig Mies van der Rohe, Neue Nationalgalerie, Berlin, 1962-1968*
bottom: *K.F. Schinkel, Altes Museum, Berlin, 1828-1830*

raum is too limited. 'Rob Krier', he writes, 'has here done a major thing. He has destroyed the Zeilenbau and restored the perimeter block.'[93] That is certainly true but Krier's main preoccupation lies elsewhere in the much more general problem of rehabilitating urban space. This does indeed imply the reintroduction of the perimeter block but it is not, as Rowe suggests, the culmination of Krier's thinking but the starting point. The desired traditional cityscape does not materialize around the perimeter block as a matter of course. The whole structure of streets and squares has to be carefully composed paying a lot of attention to the human scale of things, and this is where architecture, which gives the street and square walls their form and expression, has an essential role to play.

A striking example of irritable incomprehension is to be found in an essay by Wolfgang Pehnt about the legacy of Friedrich Schinkel.[94] The question he poses is whether historicizing architecture, or at least architecture that makes explicit use of tradition, can indeed be regarded as authentic architecture. Schinkel, who modernized the classical vocabulary in Germany in the early nineteenth century, was a self-avowed opponent of imitation and craven repetition. Pehnt comes to the conclusion that his work, however historicizing it may be, can indeed be called authentic because the classical vocabulary has been applied in a totally original way, a feat repeated in the present century by Mies van der Rohe in his design for the Neue Nationalgalerie in Berlin. This building, according to Pehnt, can be regarded as a modern version of Schinkel's Altes Museum, also in Berlin, but Mies van der Rohe, too, succeeded in interpreting his model in a highly original way.[95]

This is more than can be said for James Stirling, whose design for the Neue Staatsgalerie refers to the plan of Schinkel's Altes Museum. In Pehnt's opinion Stirling abuses Schinkel's legacy so that the museum in Stuttgart is no more than a cacophony of historicizing quotations, and the reference to Schinkel is submerged in a welter of mannerist sleights of hand whose only purpose is to astound and entertain the public.[96] Perhaps this assessment is correct, yet even so Stirling's building is unmistakably and even exceptionally original. Pehnt is looking for a normative formula, a truth, and for an aesthetic and architectural legitimacy that does not exist. Schinkel, Mies van der Rohe and Stirling have very different views about the significance of architectural heritage but none of them can lay claim, as the only true heir, to the essence of architecture.

Rob Krier, according to Pehnt has also been guilty of a completely unacceptable reworking of one of Schinkel's designs. This building, a large dwelling in the southern part of the Berlin Friedrichstadt district, was badly damaged during the Second World War and the remaining front elevation was later pulled down. In Krier's urban plan for Schinkelplatz, a relatively modest rectangular square, this façade forms one of the four walls of the square. Pehnt is very critical of Krier's reconstruction of Schinkel's façade. In fact, he argues, it is not a reconstruction at all because the new elevation deviates on numerous points from the original. This gives the reader the idea that Krier has not understood the original; Pehnt lectures him about detailing and architectural theory as if he were dealing with a failed project by a first year student.[97] Yet this analysis must be wrong, for Krier showed in *Architectural Composition* that he has an excellent grasp of

92 Julius Posener, *Berlin auf dem Wege zu einer neuen Architektur*, Munich 1979.
93 Krier 1979 (see note 79), p. 12.
94 Wolfgang Pehnt, 'Schinkel und über Schinkel hinaus', in: Wolfgang Pehnt, *Die Erfindung der Geschichte*, Munich 1989, pp. 50-63.
95 Op. cit. p. 56.
96 Op. cit. p. 59.
97 Op. cit. p. 58.

traditional details and façade compositions.

Although he does not say it in so many words, Pehnt evidently believes that a reconstruction is only legitimate when the original building is rebuilt in its totality, down to the smallest detail, and without deviating one centimetre from the historic plan and elevations. That was of course impossible in this case, for dwellings built by Schinkel and his contemporaries belong once and for all to the past. The façade reconstructed by Krier refers more to the size and scale of the prevailing urban space than to the details of Schinkel's architecture – contrary to what Pehnt thinks or would have one believe. The point of the exercise is not Karl Friedrich Schinkel's personal signature, but the typological development of Berlin housing in the nineteenth century. Rob Krier's 'reconstruction' is nothing more than one of countless variations of this type of façade to have been developed. What had once been an upper-middle-class apartment block went on to become a tenement and the same type is now deployed in social housing.

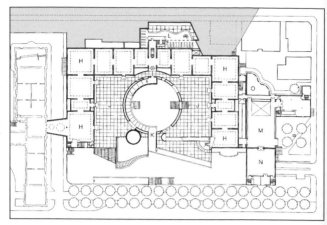

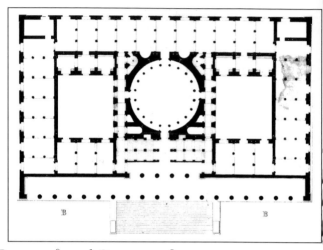

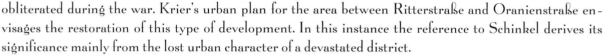

What Pehnt fails to notice is that Krier has abstracted Schinkel's façade into an urbanist element and in this context the details – as Berlage could have told him – are not of primary importance. What matters here are the broad outlines of the architectural design, the interface between architecture and urbanism. Krier is not a historicizing designer in the conventional, stylistic sense of the word – the main point is not, in his view, an architectural style as such but the reconstruction of the traditional urban space. Pehnt disregards the fact that the original perimeter development in this part of Berlin was entirely obliterated during the war. Krier's urban plan for the area between Ritterstraße and Oranienstraße envisages the restoration of this type of development. In this instance the reference to Schinkel derives its significance mainly from the lost urban character of a devastated district.

The third example of criticism, the downright hostile, merits attention because it is not directed at a concrete design but at a design method; using a mixture of ideological and historical arguments it attempts to bring a major tendency in twentieth-century urbanism into disrepute. Gerhard Fehl's ostensible target in his recent, suggestively entitled book, *Kleinstadt, Steildach, Volksgemeinschaft. Zum "reaktionären Modernismus" im Bau- und Stadtbaukunst*,[98] is Vittorio Lampugnani's 1992 'Reform and Tradition' exhibition. However, this criticism is only the opening volley in a frontal assault on those who attempted to save traditional urbanism from total collapse during the first half of the twentieth century. Now the modern movement has in turn

98 Gerhard Fehl, *Kleinstadt, Steildach, Volksgemeinschaft. Zum reaktionären Modernismus im Bau- und Stadtbaukunst*, Braunschweig/Wiesbaden 1995.

top: *James Stirling, Plan Neue Staatsgalerie, Stuttgart, 1980-1983*
bottom: *K.F. Schinkel, Plan Altes Museum Berlijn, 1828-1830*

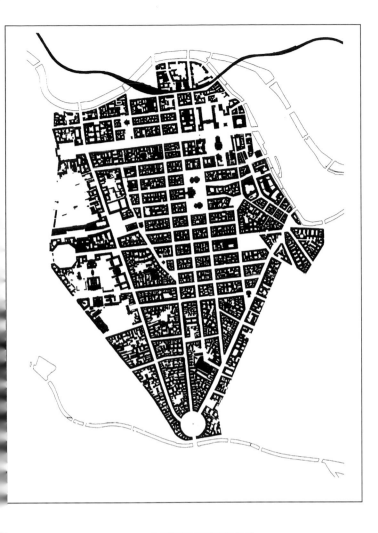

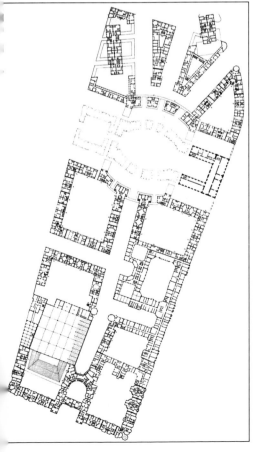

FAÇADE DES HAUSES WELCHES DER OFENFABRIKANT FEILNER IN DER HASENHEGER-GASSE IN GEBRANTER ERDE AUSGEFÜHRT HAT.

top left: Original perimeter block, Süd-Friedrichstadt, Berlin, before, 1940
bottom left: Rob Krier, Urban design of the area Ritterstrasse-Oranienstrasse, Berlin, 1977-1980
top right: Rob Krier, Dwelling Ritterstrasse, Berlin, 1980-1983
bottom right: K.F. Schinkel, Dwelling Ritterstrasse, Berlin, 1828-1829

collapsed, there has been a revival of interest in theory formation during this period, a move Fehl sees as a return to the most dubious form of political and social conservatism.

Rob Krier's name is not mentioned in Fehl's book but indirectly he, too, is in the dock. After all, *Stadtraum* was dedicated to Camillo Sitte and it is Sitte who, according to Fehl, must be regarded as the patriarch of conservative thinking in German urbanism. In 1889 this Austrian architect published a very influential book entitled *Der Städtebau nach seinen künstlerischen Grundsätzen* (Town Planning According to its Artistic Principles).[99] It was by way of a reaction to a town planning reference book that had appeared in 1876: Reinhard Baumeister's *Stadterweiterungen in technischer, baupolizeilicher und wirtschaftlicher Beziehung*.[100] The titles of both publications indicate the nature of the controversy. Baumeister was an engineer and he portrayed town planning as a purely technical and practical issue. Sitte reacted to this with an argument about the deplorable aesthetic quality of modern urban extensions compared with the beauty of the traditional urban space.

As is often the case, both writers were right. Baumeister stressed the efficient functioning of the urban organism and in particular the importance of a healthy environment. As such his arguments are strongly reminiscent of functionalist arguments in the 1920s and 1930s. He championed a generously conceived urban layout, with plenty of light and air, and he realized that modern forms of public transport made it possible to build attractive suburbs outside the densely built-up city centres. Compared with Baumeister, Sitte was indeed a traditionalist. He loathed the rigidly orthogonal modern subdivision system used for nineteenth-century urban extensions and his detailed analyses of medieval town squares indicate an unmistakable preference for the provincial atmosphere of the pre-industrial city. Many of Fehl's carefully selected quotations from Sitte confirm the impression of a somewhat parochial reaction to the rapid developments taking place in the modern metropolis.

It is indeed possible to give Sitte's rather conservative views a decidedly reactionary gloss and this is what happened in Germany. But Sitte's reception elsewhere in Europe, especially in England and the Netherlands, shows that such an interpretation is by no means inevitable. Fehl is at pains to draw a direct line from Sitte, via Karl Henrici and Paul Schultze-Naumburg, to the urbanist ideals of the German National Socialists. By thus linking Sitte to the Third Reich he attempts to demonstrate that his defence of the aesthetic quality of the traditional city leads irrevocably to unacceptable social consequences. The question is whether the German situation is truly representative for the significance of Sitte's book.

In Germany, the period 1890-1933 is still overshadowed by what happened between 1933 and 1945. Fehl proves himself a poor historian by exploiting this fact with unashamed rhetoric. In one long sentence Fehl links Lampugnani's politically blameless exhibition with *Kristallnacht*, a clear breach of the rules governing academic debate.[101] Julius Posener's verdict on German architecture and town planning between 1890 and 1914 was a good deal more subtle. He even had the courage to write approvingly of Paul Schultze-Naumburg's

Bedford Park London, 1870s

99 Camillo Sitte, *Der Städtebau nach seinen künstlerischen Grundsätzen*, Wien 1889. English translation with an in-depth historical introduction: George R. Collins, Christiane Crasemann Colins, *Camillo Sitte: The Birth of Modern Townplanning*, New York 1986 (London 1965).

100 Reinhard Baumeister, *Stadterweiterungen in technischer, baupolizeilicher und wirtschaftlicher Beziehung*, Berlin 1876.

101 Fehl 1995 (see note 98), p. 20.

books which together make up the informative series *Kulturarbeiten*.[102] This architect was a staunch supporter of National Socialism even before 1933, but as anyone reading the many volumes of *Kulturarbeiten* today will discover, perhaps to their discomfort, his view of architecture and town planning has an irresistible charm. One is forced to conclude that although Schultze-Naumburg was a political simpleton, he nevertheless had a keen eye for the gracefully aged built environment that has already managed to survive for several generations.

It is fairly easy to show that Fehl is wrong by pointing out that the reception given to Sitte's ideas in England and the Netherlands had nothing to do with a conservative vision of social life. Quite the contrary. Politically speaking both Raymond Unwin, Sitte's English advocate, and H.P. Berlage, were decidedly progressive. The sharp distinction Fehl draws between functional urbanism à la Baumeister, and aesthetic-conservative urbanism according to Sitte's principles, is almost entirely absent in England and the Netherlands. In the Netherlands there was some discussion about where to draw the line between the task of the engineer on the one hand and that of the architect on the other, but this problem was solved – in typical Dutch fashion – by consultation.[103]

Lacking a professional literature of their own, the British read German town planning handbooks: Baumeister, Sitte and Joseph Stübben's *Der Städtebau* (City Building), a hefty book published in 1890 that gave a wellnigh comprehensive picture of European town planning practice at that time.[104] This inspired T.C. Horsefall to visit Germany in 1897,[105] where he was greatly impressed by the role of government in regulating urban development and public housing. Although he was primarily interested in the housing issue, he was fully aware that town planning and housing were indissolubly connected. In 1904 he published *The Improvement of the Dwellings and Surroundings of the People: the Example of Germany*.[106]

Given his administrative interest in practical problems Horsefall was not very interested in Sitte's contribution to the town planning debate. Sitte was introduced to England by the architect Raymond Unwin. Although his book, *Town Planning in Practice*, which appeared in 1909, devoted a lot of attention to the aesthetic problems of town planning it did not neglect the practical and civil engineering aspects of the profession.[107] Yet Unwin's interest in medieval German townscapes had nothing to do with a conservative distaste for the modern metropolis. England was in the vanguard of experiments with suburbs in which the advantages of town and country did not exclude one another. The London suburb of Bedford Park, built in the 1860s, is a superb example of a village, complete with village pub and village church, in the middle of a metropolis.[108] Unwin aligned himself with this tradition, and thanks to Sitte's lucid formulation of the aesthetic principles underlying the familiar appearance of European urban spaces, he was able to devise a systematic and manageable method for designing exclusively low-rise development plans for the urban periphery.

Unwin was also very influential in the Netherlands, witness for instance G. Feenstra's book *Tuinsteden* (Garden Cities).[109] But a more interesting relationship is that between H.P. Berlage and Sitte.[110] Berlage of course owes his fame as an urbanist to his second design for Amsterdam Zuid, but by the time this plan was finished in 1915 he had already been thinking about town planning problems for more than thirty years. His

102 Posener 1979 (see note 92), chapter 'Kulturarbeiten', pp. 191-222.

103 Peter de Ruijter, *Voor volkshuisvesting en stedebouw*, Utrecht 1987, pp. 194-208.

104 Joseph Stübben, *Der Städtebau*, Darmstadt 1890, reprint Braunschweig/Wiesbaden 1980.

105 Gordon E. Cherry, *The Evolution of British Town Planning*, London 1974, p. 26.

106 T.C. Horsefall, *The Improvement of the Dwellings and Surroundings of the People: the Example of Germany*, Manchester 1904.

107 Raymond Unwin, *Town Planning in Practice*, London 1909, reprint New York 1994.

108 Mark Girouard, *Sweetness and Light. The Queen Anne Movement 1860-1900*, London 1977, pp. 160-176. See also: Helen Long, *The Edwardian House*, Manchester 1993.

109 G. Feenstra, *Tuinsteden en volkshuisvesting in Nederland en buitenland*, Amsterdam 1920.

110 Manfred Bock, *Anfänge einer neuen Architektur. Berlages Beitrag zur architektonischen Kultur der Niederlande im ausgehenden 19. Jahrhundert*, The Hague/Wiesbaden 1983, pp. 104-120; Vincent van Rossem, 'Beschouwingen over stedebouw 1892-1914', in: Sergio Polano (ed.), *Hendrik Petrus Berlage. Het complete werk*, Alphen 1988 (Milan 1987), pp. 46-66.

interest in town planning had been aroused early on by traffic problems in Amsterdam, which inspired a lecture entitled 'Amsterdam and Venice' in 1883.[111] It is clear from this lecture that Berlage regarded contemporary Paris as an ideal example of modern town planning. Nineteenth-century Paris, with its new boulevards and avenues was indeed a monumental example of improvements in circulation in combination with a striking architectural vocabulary for the new urban space.[112]

Given his marked preference for the more classical character of modern Paris, Berlage was not receptive to Sitte's rousing descriptions of medieval town squares. Nevertheless, he immediately grasped the enormous significance of Sitte's book. This is apparent from the fact that he made 'aesthetic principles' the subject of a lecture given in 1892 under the title 'Art in town planning'.[113] Berlage was interested in Sitte's percipient analysis of the way spatial effects arise from the interaction between architecture and the urban plan. From Sitte he learnt that an urban ensemble of buildings is architecturally more interesting than isolated monumentality, but he was not prepared to go along with Sitte's demand that the architectural design should be entirely subordinated to the aesthetics of the urban space. Berlage sought a solution in which the integrity of the architectural design and Sitte's basic principles could be combined without unacceptable compromises having to be made, either in the architecture or in the urban design.

It was a problem that was to pre-occupy Berlage for a long time. In the end the solution he sought gradually acquired shape in modern housing construction. Around 1900, large numbers of dwellings were built in Berlin by architects such as Alfred Messel, Paul Mebes and Albert Geßner for an increasingly prosperous middle class.[114] In the process, the nineteenth-century perimeter block, with its irritating staccato of lot divisions, was typologically transformed into a modern urban block designed as a single architectural entity. In 1908 Mebes published an instructive book entitled *Um 1800*, that identified tradition as the source of inspiration for this architecture.[115] An overview of these superb apartment buildings, compiled by Geßner, appeared a year later under the title *Das deutsche Miethaus*.[116]

In due time, practice was followed by theory. The typological revolution in housing construction in Berlin and especially its significance for town planning, was lucidly described by Walter Curt Behrendt in 1911 in his book *Die einheitliche Blockfront als Raumelement im Stadtbau*. Berlage, who had always followed developments in Germany closely, advised the director of the Amsterdam Municipal Housing Agency, Arie Keppler, to read this book. And so the groundwork was laid for the development of the Amsterdam School, the Dutch version of 'die einheitliche

UITBREIDINGSPLAN ZUID
DER
GEMEENTE AMSTERDAM
SCHAAL 1:5000

111 Bock 1983 (see note 110), p. 92.
112 David van Zanten, *Building Paris*, New York 1994.
113 Bock 1983 (see note 110), p. 104.
114 Posener 1979 (see note 92), chapter 'Das Mietshaus wandelt
     sich', pp. 319-368.
115 Paul Mebes, *Um 1800. Architektur und Handwerk im letzten
     Jahrhundert ihrer traditionellen Entwicklung*, Munich 1908,
     second edition Munich 1918.

Blockfront' (the unified block façade). As a result of Keppler's determined action, Michiel de Klerk was given the opportunity to realize his famous housing blocks in the Amsterdam Spaarndammer district during the First World War.[117]

Thanks to De Klerk's brilliant prototypes, it was not long before a method was developed in Amsterdam that allowed for perfect coordination of urban plan and buildings – and thus for the exemplary manner in which Berlage's development plan was realized. After De Klerk's untimely death in the autumn of 1923, it was Berlage who first drew attention to the significance of his architecture, for the 'Amsterdam school of thought' had made it literally possible to give shape to new urban extensions. Four years after De Klerk's death Berlage tried in vain to explain to the participants of the first CIAM congress, that the Amsterdam model, where clients, architects and government worked together smoothly, was ideal for solving urbanist and architectural problems. But they were not interested; their minds were already dazzled by the radical ideas of the modern movement.

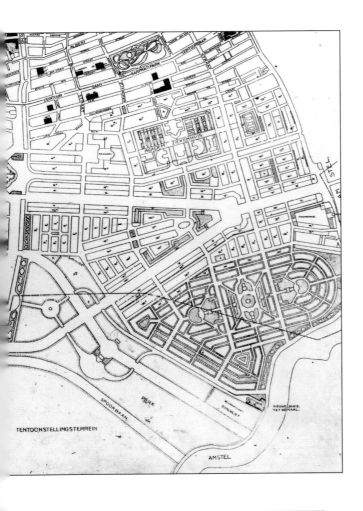

116 Albert Gessner, *Das deutsche Miethaus. Ein Beitrag zur Städtekultur der Gegenwart*, Munich 1909.
117 Vincent van Rossem, 'Architektuur en stad in 1913: de overstap van bouwkunst naar stedebouw', in: Jan de Vries (ed.), *Nederland 1913. Een reconstructie van het culturele leven*, Amsterdam/Haarlem 1988, pp. 132-154.

top: H.P. Berlage, Second design for Amsterdam-Zuid, 1915
right: Block 2, Spaarndammerplantsoen, Amsterdam, 1914-1916

Berlage, Dudok, Weeber

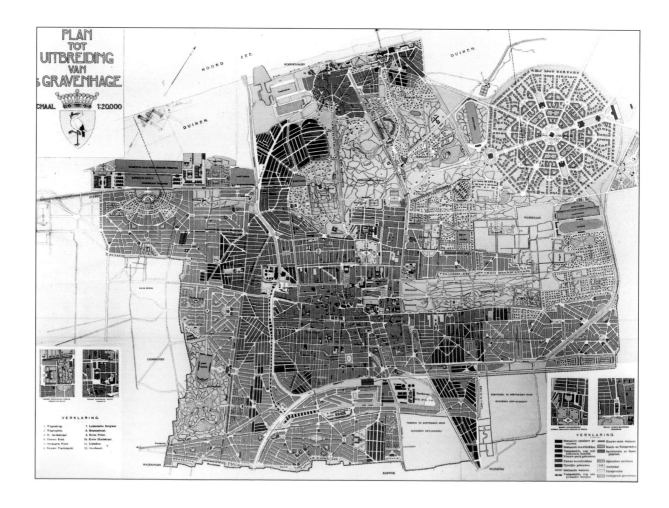

The making of a new commercial centre

By the time the effects of the transport revolution generated by the steam-engine had started to have an impact on urban traffic some hundred and fifty years ago, European cities were already living on borrowed time. The crux of the problem is not, as is generally assumed, the space taken up by modern road traffic. The greatest devourer of space is the motorcar, yet by the time car ownership had begun to assume a mass character (not until after the Second World War in Europe), traditional city life had already all but disappeared and cities were functioning in a radically new way. The process had begun in London where a new form of urban life began to develop in the early nineteenth century thanks to a rapidly growing urban rail network. The Underground made it possible for people to live in attractive outer suburbs, that is to say in a trim, single-family dwelling with garden, and to work in the centre of the city.[1]

Now that it has once again become fashionable to live in the old inner cities (proof of relative prosperity and good taste), the wholesale flight from the centre of the city is less automatic than it used to be. Today it is wellnigh impossible to form a realistic picture of the extremely high densities that were once the norm in European cities and whereby dwelling, work, recreation and transportation were a complete chaos, the drainage of severely polluted waste water was left largely to chance and the air was thick with the equally heavily polluted smoke of innumerable chimneys. The mere fact that mortality rates were considerably lower in the suburbs made them a more attractive option than the centre of the city. On top of this, they also offered a socially modern environment. The ghostly historical street scene, populated by a pre-industrial underclass of ragged wretches, might have been a popular literary theme, but it was certainly not considered a suitable backdrop to clean middle-class family life.[2]

The exodus from old London and the tremendous growth of commercial services in the city centre, resulted in a comprehensive reconstruction of the historic heart of the city. London had been rebuilt once before, after the Great Fire in the seventeenth century, but the advent of the Underground in the nineteenth century made it possible to build a new centre, a monofunctional office district.[3] At the same time new, equally monofunctional residential areas sprang up. Moreover, the trend towards ever-bigger ships signalled the disappearance of the dock industry from the centre of London. The upshot of all these

---

H.P. Berlage, Development plan, The Hague, 1908

1 Donald Olsen, *The Growth of Victorian London*, London 1976.
2 Gertrude Himmelfarb, *The Idea of Poverty. England in the Early Industrial Age*, New York 1983.
3 John Summerson, 'The Victorian Rebuilding of the City of London', in: John Summerson, *The Unromantic Castle*, London 1990, pp. 193-216.

developments was a functionally dispersed city. A similar trend became visible in American cities like New York, Chicago and Los Angeles around the turn of the century.

In the Netherlands, where the changes wrought by the industrial revolution were relatively late in making themselves felt, it was some time before decentralization set in. Nonetheless, Amsterdam, too, had to contend with a veritable exodus of affluent citizens to the new residential areas in the east (*het Gooi*) and the coastal area to the west. It was certainly no accident that H.P. Berlage began his career in Amsterdam with a lecture, entitled 'Amsterdam and Venice', about the relationship between town planning and traffic problems.[4] Core-formation and road traffic have been inseparable right from the word go. Berlage felt that the municipal authorities were trying to solve the problem with makeshift measures, such as filling in canals and replacing the stone arched bridges with bridges that were more suited to modern trams – a flat road surface supported by iron beams. What was lacking, as he saw it, was a monumental vision complete with major swaths like the *percements* Haussmann had employed in his reconstruction of Paris.

Fortunately, the historic inner cities of the Netherlands were all a bit too small for urban major interventions à la Haussmann. But although developments in the Netherlands were on a smaller scale, they were no less dynamic. The appearance of The Hague, for instance, changed out of all recognition in a relatively short time. Today it is difficult to imagine that the Hague townscape was once characterized by a girdle of canals typical of Dutch cities in this part of the Netherlands. Old photographs of the Spui and Nieuwe Haven reveal a townscape more reminiscent of the Amsterdam canal zone than of modern-day The Hague. Many canals, including Herengracht and Fluwelen Burgwal, had already been filled in for hygienic reasons at the beginning of the nineteenth century. Increasing traffic congestion prompted a second wave of canal-filling at the beginning of the twentieth century, at which time the Houtmarkt and Turfmarkt waterways also disappeared. Thus a characteristic part of the historic city had already been sacrificed to modernization quite early on.

What did not disappear, however, was the social division so typical of The Hague.[5] On the contrary, it was if anything exacerbated. The simple historical division between the village of The Hague, clustered around the Grote Kerk, and the court to the north of the village, evolved into a much more extensive functional specialization of city quarters in the course of nineteenth century. On the western side of the city, attractively situated on the higher dune land, new residential areas sprang up to meet the needs of the growing corps of civil servants. The old village burgeoned into a modern shopping centre, while an industrial town complete with working-class neighbourhoods materialized on the eastern edge of The Hague. This geographical separation of functions was not, of course, entirely fortuitous.

4   Manfred Bock, *Anfänge einer neuen Architektur. Berlages Beitrag zur architektonischen Kultur der Niederlande im ausgehenden 19. Jahrhundert*, The Hague/Wiesbaden 1983, p. 92.
5   Maarten van Doorn, 'Een verhaal van twee steden, Den Haag tot 1890', in: Victor Freyser (ed.), *Het veranderend stadsbeeld van Den Haag, 1890-1990*, Zwolle 1990, pp. 9-30; Henk Schmal, *Den Haag of 's-Gravenhage?*, Utrecht 1995.

The Spuikwartier

The lower-lying polder land to the east of the city was less in demand as a residential area. Moreover, transport and industry had always been concentrated on this side of the city where the Trekvliet canal provided the major passenger and goods link with other cities in the region. The Spuikwartier (Spui district) had for centuries functioned as a sort of docks area for inland shipping. With the arrival of the railways – likewise on the eastern side of the city – traditional industries gradually evolved into modern industrial enterprises. The result was a district the better-off denizen of The Hague had little reason to visit. In 1893 an observer noted the sharp dividing line separating rich and poor in The Hague, a city which 'can be readily divided into two halves, into an upper and a lower half each of a very different nature: if one draws a line from west to east that begins at Loosduinse Brug, continues along Riviervismarkt and through the Passage, Poten and Herengracht and finishes at the end of Bezuidenhoutse Weg, one will have more or less separated the hereditary and financial aristocracy, the neighbourhoods of the wealthy and well-to-do, of the respectable civil servants and military personnel, from the commercial areas, the shopping precinct and the poorer neighbourhoods.'[6]

The old Spuikwartier was in a particularly sorry state. Here, within the former girdle of canals, scores of sub-standard dwellings had sprung up cheek by jowl during the nineteenth century. There was no planning to speak of and today it would simply be called a slum. Old maps of the area reveal in its south-eastern corner, bordered by Nieuwe Haven, Uilebomen, Oranje Buitensingel, Herengracht and Fluwelen Burgwal, a veritable island of poverty that is not even served by normal streets. The conditions here were quite appalling, worse even than anything encountered in the notorious Jordaan district of Amsterdam, and it is no exaggeration to say that the Spuikwartier as a whole, bordered by Stationsstraat and Wagenstraat, Spuistraat, Poten, Herengracht and the Singel canals, had become a dilapidated, run-down but over-crowded part of town. In other words, by the turn of the century, The Hague already had a district in dire need of renewal.

In the previous paragraph, a comparison was made with the Jordaan district in Amsterdam. This, too, was a very old residential area with a lot of industry which had become riddled with narrow alleyways during the nineteenth century as it struggled to accommodate the influx of rural immigrants coming to seek their fortune in the fast-growing urban labour market. But the Jordaan's characteristic street grid formed a very solid urban structure so that slums could only develop on the inside of the existing perimeter blocks. Later on the narrow lanes could be demolished without affecting the basic urban structure of the neighbourhood. To the extent that there was a half-way solid structure in the Spuikwartier in The Hague, the result was much the same. But where there was no pre-existing structure any slum clearance programme necessarily entailed the development of a totally new urbanistic vision for the area. In the Spuikwartier, only the former building lines along Herengracht and Fluwelen Burgwal survived the ravages of time; urban dynamics gradually erased the slum area behind them and as far as Uilebomen.

The first assault on this amorphous district was launched by Berlage. His extension plan for The Hague,

6   Cited in Van Doorn 1990 (see note 5), p. 9.

dated 1908, shows a new thoroughfare (today's Grote Marktstraat) linking Prinsegracht and the Spui, while to the north of the Spui a link has been created with Kalvermarkt thus producing a through road between Prinsegracht and Fluwelen Burgwal. More or less in passing, the dead-end Muzenstraat has been extended to Fluwelen Burgwal. In his explanatory notes Berlage commented: 'if, finally, a road is cut between Fluwelen Burgwal and Zwarteweg, at the same time making use of the alleyway beside the Infermerie and Muzenstraat, the result is a direct link with the railway terminal of the State Railways, a link that will retain its importance even should the latter disappear.'[7]

Berlage's remark about the possible disappearance of the State Railways terminal, the present Central Station, is a reference to his proposal to combine the two Hague railway terminals on the site of the Hollandse Spoor station; he had prophetically foreseen that Central Station would otherwise present an enormous obstacle to urban development in The Hague. His successor as municipal town planning adviser, W.M. Dudok, had another go at removing this obstacle shortly after the Second World War but he, too, failed. In retrospect, of course, it is easy to see that Berlage and Dudok were right, but such radical proposals are notoriously difficult to implement. A similar problem in Amsterdam was solved around 1930, thanks to the determination of the then director of the *Dienst der Publiek Werken* (Office of Public Works), W.A. de Graaf.[8]

In the event Central Station was neither demolished nor moved underground as Berlage and Dudok had advised, and this has indeed had far-reaching consequences for core-formation in the Spuikwartier. Nevertheless, the process of core-formation had already begun with Berlage's projected Prinsegracht-Grote Marktstraat-Kalvermarkt-Fluwelen Burgwal *percement*. In 1912 the city council formally decided to go ahead with this expensive undertaking and the first new buildings appeared in the 1920s. The development of Grote Marktstraat was reasonably successful but on the northern side of the Spui, on Kalvermarkt, new development was a good deal tardier. The first building was not erected until 1936. This was A.J. Kropholler's department store for the home furnishing concern Hulshoff; although the firm still exists, the building has since disappeared. The Depression and the ensuing war put paid to the planned *percement* between the Spui and Fluwelen Burgwal with the result that the area fell victim to a process of continuous neglect and continuous demolition – including the occasional new building – which did not stop until the majority of the buildings around Kalvermarkt and Turfmarkt and on either side of Muzenstraat, were razed to the ground in 1975.

7   H.P. Berlage, 'Het Uitbreidingsplan van 's-Gravenhage', in: *Bouwkunst*, 1 (1909) no. 4/5 (July-September), p. 128.
8   'Rapport betreffende de verbetering van de spoorwegtoestanden in Amsterdam Oost', in: *Amsterdams gemeenteblad* 1933, pt. 1, Appendix B.

top: *W.M. Dudok, Reconstruction plan Bezuidenhout and development plan for the Spui, The Hague, 1947*
bottom: *J.J. Hornstra, J.G.W. Luyt, J.H. Munnik, H.C.P. Nuyten and P. Verhave, Plan 2000, The Hague, 1949*

From Dudok to Weber

The first official plan for large-scale renovation of the Spuikwartier was prepared by Dudok within the framework of postwar reconstruction. Almost simultaneously there appeared 'Plan 2000', a project worked out during the war by five Hague architects. The contrast between the two plans was considerable. In his design notes Dudok spoke about 'inserting' and 're-creating': 'In general these two concepts', he claimed, 'characterize this type of urban design work; re-creation is possible only within a very limited framework and in such a context the art of town planning is never anything else or anything more than the art of the attainable.'[9] These were the words of an experienced urbanist who had moreover never felt much sympathy for the radical tendency in architecture and urbanism. 'Plan 2000' on the other hand envisaged a total

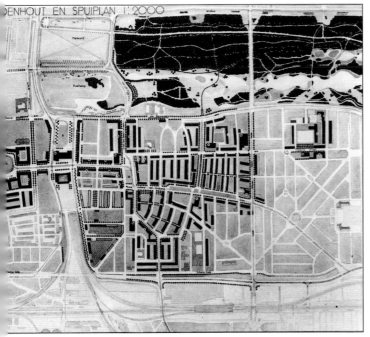

reconstruction of The Hague, an exercise that was based on the most radical theoretical principles of the pre-war CIAM. Owing to an unfortunate combination of circumstances, Dudok's well-balanced plan was never executed and although its pre-war ideas were the subject of fierce debate within CIAM itself, the ludicrous notions contained in 'Plan 2000' exerted more and more influence on municipal town planning policies.[10]

It is certainly worthwhile taking a closer look at Dudok's plan. His scenario for rebuilding Bezuidenhout, a bombed-out residential area to the north of Central Station, is less relevant to our purposes than a related slum-clearance plan he had drawn up for the Spuikwartier, an area bordered by Kalvermarkt, Muzenstraat, Zwarteweg, Uilebomen and the Spui. Dudok's plan was obviously an elaboration of Berlage's projected *percements*, but he had a clearer vision of the future function of the area. Immediately to the south of the extended Muzenstraat Dudok placed a number of new ministerial buildings around a large square. He spoke of a 'new centre of government', and argued that 'it is important that the countless citizens who visit government offices every day should not have to travel great distances within the city on top of a long train journey.'[11]

In other words, Dudok foresaw fairly large-scale core-formation and felt that the presence of a railway station was essential in this context. From an urban planning point of view, the new centre of government, dubbed 'Plein 1945' (1945 Square) by Dudok, was also exceptionally well embedded in the surrounding street plan. The manner in which this was done attests unmistakably to talent, experience and genuine town planning expertise. The new

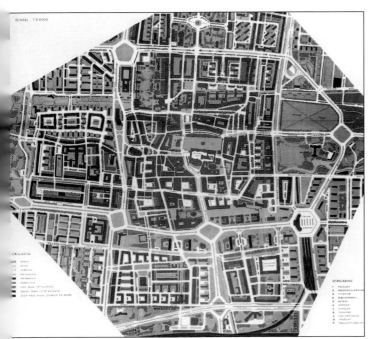

9 W.M. Dudok, Gemeente 's-Gravenhage, *Twee herbouwplannen voor 's-Gravenhage*, Den Haag 1946, p. 6.
10 Irene van Huik, 'Dudok en Den Haag in de jaren 1930-1950', in: Freyser 1990 (see note 5), pp. 99-142; Michelle Provoost, 'Den Haag in de jaren 1950-1970', in: Freyser 1990 (see note 5), pp. 143-188.
11 Dudok 1946 (see note 9), p. 8.

Kalvermarkt – already projected by Berlage but as yet unbuilt – forms a link with the Spui on the north-west side of Plein 1945 and on the southern side the Spui is accessible via Schedeldoekshaven and Ammunitiehaven. On the eastern flank a wide road runs over the Oranje Buitensingel and over a new, underground Central Station, to the rebuilt Bezuidenhout. The result is a balanced urban plan with an almost classical air. In strictly functional terms, the east-west link between the Spui and Bezuidenhout can be compared with the projected and partially constructed Prins Bernhard viaduct of later date, but what is strikingly clear from such a comparison is the difference between genuine urbanism and the vandalism that was so characteristic of later *structuurplannen* (structural plans), which blithely ignored the urban space as a three-dimensional, architectural and aesthetic problem.

Dudok's vision of the reconstruction of The Hague was criticized as 'conservative' by his colleagues, who included J.H. van den Broek and C. Van Eesteren. It was, quite simply, unfashionable to design beautiful squares and attractive cityscapes. On the other hand, in his perception of the development of the city he was way ahead of his time. Dudok was in favour of decentralizing core functions. In order to facilitate this he had projected an underground rail loop running from Central Station in a wide arc along the western flank of the city. The space was there and had this infrastructural amenity been realized shortly after the war and hence for a modest price, it would have been possible to spread the effects of core-formation in The Hague and to prevent the frenetic concentration of huge office buildings around Central Station. The Amsterdam orbital railway, a town planning item budgeted for in the *Algemeen Uitbreidingsplan* (General Extension Plan) of 1934, proves that Dudok was right.

Unfortunately, criticism of Dudok's plans was not confined to colleagues blinded by ideology. The city council was not happy with his idea of decentralizing core functions – they could not of course imagine that at some time in the distant future they would be dealing with hundreds of thousands of square metres of office space. The national government was equally deaf to plans for a new centre of government in the Spuikwartier – which has since become a fact, but without the benefit of any urban planning vision. Politicians and officials were curiously fearful that such a centre might compete with the genuine centre of – political – power around the Binnenhof and consequently opted for dispersal of government buildings. It is a melancholy thought that the tremendous concentration of bureaucratic office space around Central Station, space that in the usual fashion has been treated as a mass product, should have been the indirect result of the mobility policy. Lastly, Dudok's visionary rail loop was rejected by the *Nederlandse Spoorwegen* (Dutch Railways), a company that in the ensuing decades almost succeeded in destroying itself because of its total lack of vision regarding the future of passenger transport.

Once Dudok's ideas had been tor-

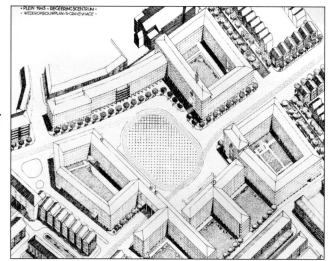

left: W.M. Dudok, Aerial perspective, 'Plein 1945',
The Hague, 1946
middle: Master plan, The Hague, 1957

pedoed, the question remaining was: what now? The national government's unwillingness to make large-scale investments in a government centre that might have revitalized the Spuikwartier, made it extremely difficult for the city council to steer the process of demolition and core-formation set in motion by Berlage in the right direction. In this dilemma the problem of car traffic infrastructure unfortunately acquired a key role. Because public transport remained mute and was in any case not taken seriously by modern urbanism, the idea that the construction of a grid of city motorways would improve the quality of city life was able to take hold. In this context, 'Plan 2000' suddenly seemed to show the way forward.

Closer inspection of 'Plan 2000' reveals that the historical aspect of The Hague had scarcely figured in the planners's deliberations. The plan's real premises are wholly abstract: the idea of a strict motorway grid in combination with a completely one-dimensional view of the way cities function. In the centre of this utopian Hague, corralled in a straitjacket of motor traffic, it is still possible to recognize something, though not much, of the historic inner city. But the Spuikwartier and the Schilderswijk have had to make way for strange urbanist fantasies where the motorcar is the noisy victor. A thorough and genuinely critical analysis of these modernist hallucinations has still to be written – the inhuman, totalitarian character gives particular pause for thought – but 'Plan 2000' finally brought the urbanist problems in the Spuikwartier to a head.

The period between Dudok's plan for the Spuikwartier, in 1946, and that of Carel Weeber in 1982, can only be described as a disastrous low point in the urban development of The Hague. When it finally became clear that public transport was not going to insist upon a major role, the motorcar automatically stepped into the breach. The structural plan presented in 1957 was strongly reminiscent of 'Plan 2000' in that it had been designed according to pre-war CIAM principles – division of functions and free passage for the motorcar. All the core functions were concentrated in the inner city and a circle immediately around it. The residential function in this area, which included a large part of the Spuikwartier and the Schilderswijk, had been entirely sacrificed to core-formation. Projected around this new business centre was the inner ring, an urban motorway of generous proportions.

These plans were the *coup de grâce* for Dudok's scenario for the Spuikwartier. On a scale-model produced by the city council in 1956 to show the building plans for offices on Kalvermarkt and Turfmarkt, the was no trace of the original buildings. Dudok's urbanist subtleties had as good as vanished: the urban space, still a well thought-out whole in his plan, had completely disintegrated. Only the trees on the model gave some definition to the public space, but in fact what we have here is the familiar modernist no man's land punctuated by a random scattering of buildings. This dispiriting picture is a fairly accurate reflection of what later happened between the Nieuwe Kerk and Central Station. Yet it is to some extent a flattering picture, for the Prins Bernhard viaduct, the height of urbanist folly, was still conspicuous by its absence.

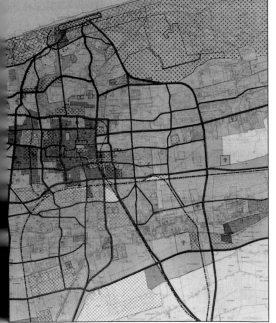

Since that time many plans have been drawn up for the area but the leit-motif has remained car traffic and core-formation. The city's town planning policy, which had still seemed so modern in 1957, gradually fossilized within a bureaucratic structure that with the passing years began to exhibit signs of

Model, Spuikwartier, The Hague, 1956

increasingly serious forms of hardening of the arteries. A structural plan presented in 1970, for example, differed scarcely at all from the 1957 design. The Spuikwartier and the Schilderswijk were still viewed as old-fashioned residential areas and as such ripe for demolition and ideal for future core-formation. The eastern part of the inner ring consisted of a thick red line mercilessly intent on carving out a route that would allow motor traffic free passage between the eastern and western sides of the new business centre situated to the east of the historic inner city.

Even so, an attentive observer could have detected as far back as 1970 that a change of direction in urbanist thinking was in the air. While it was gradually becoming clear that the blessings of the motocar were bound to lead to insoluble problems in the long term, it was also beginning to dawn on people that the dilapidation and the wholesale demolition of old urban housing areas had a fatal effect on the urban economy, which operates quite differently and is much more complex than the modernists, with their large-scale delusions, had realized.[12] The deportation of inner-city residents to distant satellite towns like Zoetermeer, Purmerend and Almere meant that the retail sector and the cultural facilities in the old urban centres no longer had any basis of support. Just as the first contours of a more balanced approach to traffic management were starting to become visible, an administrative basis was also being laid for future urban renewal programmes.

In 1967, at a congress on 'mobility under threat', the professional transporters, united in the Koninklijke Nederlandse Vereniging van Transportondernemingen (Royal Association of Transport Companies), set the ball rolling with a plea for better public transport. A year later the Ministry of Housing, Spacial Planning and Environment published a memorandum entitled 'The future of the old housing stock'. The Dutch Railways were quick to draw attention to the issue of mobility; with its 1969 memorandum 'Spoor naar 75' ('Track to 75'), the company set the come-back of public transport on the rails. The city of Amsterdam also reacted promptly to the government memorandum on old housing stock. In October 1969 the city council published a detailed memorandum entitled 'Urban renewal – preparations'. The new policy on mobility and urban renewal was to result in a totally new approach to town planning.

Town planners themselves were slowly starting to realize that city dwellers were complex beings. When they finally took the trouble to ask citizens what they thought of town planning it became apparent that the ideal modern individual envisaged by CIAM did not exist. Initially the experts had great difficulty taking the conservatism of local residents seriously. In the first round of urban renewal plans they proffered one proposal after another aimed at radically altering the existing subdivision – with the best of intentions of course, namely, to pave the way for modern and better housing. They were greatly surprised when it turned out – in the Amsterdam Dapperbuurt, for example – that this was not at all what the locals wanted: they preferred perimeter blocks surrounded by the old familiar streets. With hindsight one can see that such well-meant 'improvements' to the nineteenth-century subdivisions have produced cluttered and unwieldy results. A comparison between the street plans of the Schilderswijk in The Hague before and after urban renewal speaks volumes.

It serves no purpose to point the finger at anyone in particular. It was a time of general confusion. The urban develop-

12 Jane Jacobs, *Cities and the Wealth of Nations. Principles of Economic Life*, New York 1984.

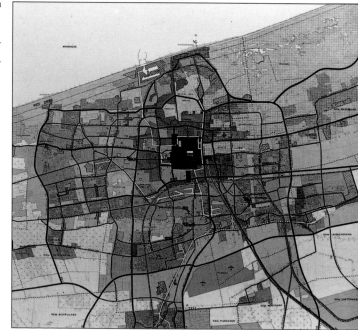

ment policy that had been pursued since the war was suddenly out of favour and new priorities were being established. Bright young politicians quickly grasped the fact that 'building for the neighbourhood' was the right way to tackle the problem but they did not, of course, know how to achieve this in terms of planning and architecture. Urbanism in particular remained unhelpfully silent at this critical moment. This discipline, it turned out, had evolved such a one-sided, one-dimensional vision of the city that its practitioners were incapable of changing tack. In the whole of the Netherlands there was not a single urban designer with the slightest inkling about historical land division plans. In the end it was the young architects who, by trial and error, and in consultation with local residents, devised a method of sorts for urban renewal. As far as The Hague is concerned, the 1970 structural plan can be regarded as the mausoleum of modern urbanism.

The failure of urbanism meant that politicians and architects were more or less condemned to work together in the 'new-style' urban development. The first politician who understood this situation, and deliberately went on to make a name for himself with an architectural policy, was the former Hague alderman Adri Duivesteijn. He first joined the city council in 1974 as the representative – long-haired and informally clad – of the neighbourhood/action-group movement. At first his notion of urban development was the fairly modest one of 'building for the neighbourhood': in other words, sound and affordable housing in familiar surroundings. But his fellow party-member on the council, Joop ten Velden, was an architect and moreover maintained good contacts with a study group of critical Hague architects calling themselves 'Werkgroep Dooievaar'.[13] Thus was the basis laid for a new architecture in The Hague.

Around the time that Duivesteijn was taking his seat on the city council, the Rijksgebouwendienst (Government Buildings Department) managed, within the space of a few years, to commit a series of blunders as a result of which the chaotic process of core-formation in The Hague reached a veritable climax. Having purchased land on a grand scale in what had become a depressingly empty-looking area between Central Station and the Spui, the Rijksgebouwendienst proceeded to erect two new government buildings for the Ministries of the Interior and of Justice (1974-1978). The orientation of these two

interlinked office buildings is peculiar to say the least but in fact one can scarcely speak of 'orientation' since they were not part of any decent urban plan. This lack of interest in the urban environment is also evident in the architecture: the urbanite at ground level is treated with sovereign disdain. The authoritarian features of the traditional ministerial building have vanished only to be replaced by an office building that would be more at home in the anonymous surroundings of the motorway. Typologically this architecture is all of a piece with the Prins Bernhard viaduct that was built at almost the same time – they are all echoes of long defunct urbanist and architectural ideas.

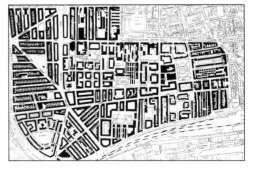

13 Richard Kleinegris, 'Den Haag in de jaren 1970-1980', in: Freyser 1990 (see note 5), pp. 189-234.

left: Master plan, The Hague, 1970
right: Street layout, Schilderswijk (before and after urban renewal), The Hague

This drama was repeated on a somewhat larger scale on the other side of Central Station, in Bezuiden-hout. During the 1970s a number of autistic colossi grouped around a multi storey car park arose on the plots that were reserved for government ministries poached from Dudok's projected residential area. As a result superb public services such as the Koninklijke Bibliotheek (National Library of the Netherlands) and the Algemeen Rijksarchief (General State Archives) were hidden away behind Central Station where the urbanite looks in vain for anything even slightly resembling urban space. The only approach to this area, according to one Hague city planner, is 'via the most miserable station exit and a hike through back streets. Every day thousands of people walk to their place of work between the loading and unloading bays of the Babylon shopping complex, via the narrow lanes between the Ministry of Foreign Affairs, the Koninklijke Bibliotheek and the Rijksarchief in the direction of the Utrechtse Baan.'[14] Quite by accident a sort of government building centre has indeed sprung up, a monster that makes one long for Dudok's Plein 1945.

While the Rijksgebouwendienst was busy creating square metres in this rather vandalistic manner and the Dienst Stadsontwikkeling (Urban Development Department) staggered on like a headless chicken, Duivesteijn and Ten Velden started their long march through the municipal bureaucracy, an archipelago of administrative empires. In the first instance they focused on urban renewal. The Third Policy Document on Planning (1973-1979) had solved the problem of how to finance this urbanist giga-project: charge the whole lot to the taxpayer's account. The two youthful politicians could therefore pursue their opposition without fear of financial counterarguments. They criticized the Dienst Stadsontwikkeling's lack of vision, its slow, not to say grudging reaction to the unprecedented possibilities offered by the Third Policy Document and they suggested creating a new department to deal with urban renewal, one that would be virtually independent of the existing bureaucratic organization.

Partly because of the construction of the series of government buildings to the east of Central Station, nothing much happened on the Spui side. The Prins Bernhard viaduct – one element of the never-completed inner ring projected in the old structural plans – was built, shortly followed by office buildings for the Interior and Justice ministries. But nobody was very clear about where to go from here. There was a plan dating from 1970, entitled 'De Nieuwe Hout' (The New Wood), that provided for large-scale core-formation, but it had expired on the drawing table due to lack of interest on the part of investors and developers. It is typical of the ineptitude of town planning policy at this time that the debate about the Spuikwartier should have been reopened by a furious conflict in the city council about a tram route.

The debate about tram routes related to the building of a raised plateau for trams and buses above the platforms of Central Station. This futuristic but, all things considered, disastrous urbanist element, entailed building viaducts around

14 Peter Verschuren, 'Het verschuivende centrum van Den Haag', in: de Architect, 24 (1993) no. 10, p. 36.

Aerial photograph of the area between Central Station and the Spui in The Hague, with a view of the Ministries of Home Affairs and Justice, early 1980s

the station to take the trams up and down. One of these viaducts, according to the plan, would sweep stylishly around Babylon before setting course, via Koekamp and Prinssegracht, for Scheveningen. 'Werkgroep Dooievaar' was vehemently opposed to this fly-over in the middle of the urban greenery and put forward alternative solutions. After years of interminable discussion it was finally decided in 1976 that the tramline in question would be routed not over Central Station but along the western flank of the station via a loop through the Spuikwartier.[15] At Ten Velden's insistence, Carel Weeber was subsequently asked to take a look at the tram route through the Spuikwartier. So it was that, almost by accident, a permanent solution for the sorely afflicted Spuikwartier seemed to be within sight at long last.

The building block as urban element

Weeber had been professor of architecture at Delft University of Technology since 1973 and in that function he had thought long and seriously about an urbanist and architectural alternative for the perverse distortion of Forum ideas that is usually labelled 'Nieuwe Truttigheid' ('new tweeness') – speed-ramp protected residential areas, cute Hansel and Gretel houses, an abundance of railway sleepers and cauliflower structures instead of subdivision plans. Along the way he had discovered the tremendous typological significance of the perimeter block: housing with a metropolitan character, which is to say of impressive size and boasting a fair number of storeys.[16] In Weeber's architectural practice this resulted in a clutch of large and generally controversial housing complexes. Nonetheless, the request to take a look at line 9's route through the Spuikwartier culminated in a vision of inner-city development that represents a turning point in the postwar history of Dutch architecture.

Weeber did not confine himself to looking at the disputed tram route, his actual brief, but also analysed the whole planning process for the Spuikwartier. His verdict was scathing. The mere siting of functional buildings in a functional traffic space, he contended, had obviously failed to generate an urban space that the average city dweller could recognize and understand. The commissioned study of tram traffic in the Spuikwartier was thus packaged in a sketch for an alternative urban plan for the area between the Spui, the Prins Bernhard viaduct, Central Station, Muzenstraat and Kalvermarkt. Not only was it possible to discern the outlines of a permanent solution in this 1977 sketch, it also served to float an urbanist idea, namely the reintroduction of the perimeter block and the mixing of residential and core functions, that was entirely new for the debate about architecture and town planning at that time.

Weeber explained the basic principles of this approach in an article entitled 'Formal objectivity in urbanism and architecture as an element of rational planning' published in late 1979. He ended his discourse with several basic observations under the heading 'Back to an autonomous urban design plan'. Weeber was clearly trying to redefine the concept of the urban design plan in such a way that it would also produce visual quality. But he did not make things any easier for himself by striving for a fairly strict division of responsibilities between urbanism and architecture. In the last instance, the problem of quality is a borderline affair. In traditional urbanism, and even more so in the splendid German word 'Stadtbaukunst' (civil art), city build-

---

15 Ed Taverne, *Carel Weeber*, Rotterdam 1989.

ing and architecture are one and the same thing. The architectural tradition was so dominant in former times that the design of urban space could count on typological coherence, added to which there was usually also a measure of stylistic coherence.

It is something of this historical dialogue between urbanism and architecture that Weeber is referring to in the following comment: 'The plan is primarily a formal, objective, two-dimensional composition, aimed at ordering public urban space, whose forms are associated with visual types entrenched in the culture of urbanism and architecture.'[16] The sting here is probably in the tail, for 'entrenched visual types' must surely refer to streets and squares. These, after all, are the spatial forms in which urbanism and architecture have for centuries and with apparent ease, formed a united whole. Weeber, however, is evidently not yet prepared to be so specific. This unwillingness to put his finger on the sore spot is most conspicuous when Weeber first boldly sweeps aside the affliction of the functional city – the traffic problem – only to remark in a sort of footnote that everything must function properly, including the traffic.

'The plan is indifferent', so his argument goes, 'to the future pattern of functions. Hence the dimensions, for example, should be geared primarily to the generation of formal visual quality, and not so much to functions (such as traffic functions). These and other functions should, however, be adequately catered for at a later stage.'[17] It is obvious that the amorphous urban space of the functional city is being brought into question here. It is simply not possible to design streets and squares so long as planning is dominated by the traffic function. If you continue to insist that traffic be able to function adequately, the question arises as to what, precisely, is meant by 'adequately'. Is this not a case of 'you can't have your cake and eat it too'?

The odd thing is that in his urban design sketch for the Spuikwartier, Weeber made it fairly clear that there was scarcely any room for car. The projected development consisted of large, entirely closed blocks and some of the streets were particularly narrow. Evidently the visual quality furnished by 'entrenched visual types' is an urban design privilege reserved for those urbanites who move about on foot. Although Weeber had no brief at this stage to produce an urban development plan, his urbanist supplement to the requested tram route study probably set many people thinking. For the first time there was a scenario that denied that the process of core-formation necessarily entailed sacrificing the spatial quality of the city to car traffic. Weeber had demonstrated that the new Spuikwartier, with a few stratagems and despite core-formation, could form a harmonious whole with the historic Hague inner city.

After Herman Hertzberger, Wim Quist and Weeber had taken part in a limited competition to draw up a development plan for the Spuikwartier, the original 1970s' tram-route discussion had a remarkably positive sequel. At Duivesteijn's insistence – he was now an alderman – Weeber's plan was chosen; the 1977 sketch could now be fleshed out into a full-fledged allocation plan and was eventually presented to the council in March 1982. At the same time it became clear that the plan area included a number of elements that severely restricted the designer's freedom. The Prins Bernhard viaduct, even in its partially demolished form, remained a dominant feature of the urban struc-

16 Carel Weeber, 'Formele objectiviteit in stedebouw en architectuur als onderdeel van rationele planning', in: *Plan* 1979, no. 11, p. 35.

17 Ibid.

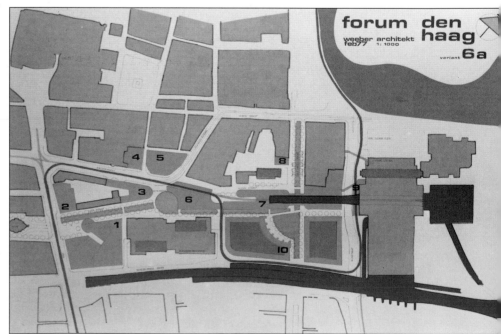

ture, as did the infrastructure for tram traffic between Kalvermarkt and the roof of Central Station. Weeber's idea of building over this viaduct and thereby hiding it from view was of course a brilliant intervention. The shape of the lot where Richard Meier's city hall/library now stands was an immutable fact within the existing street pattern, and the outward appearance of another lot had already been determined by the building of the office blocks for the ministries of the Interior and Justice.

Nonetheless, a comparison between the 1977 sketch and the 1982 allocation plan reveals that even within such a limited framework there was still a lot that needed to be designed. One big difference was the treatment of the link between the Spui and Rijnstraat – the so-called Turfmarkt route. In 1977 this was still a succession of more or less autonomous urban spaces, whereas the allocation plan was dominated by a twenty-two-metre-wide tree-filled pedestrian mall running in an almost straight line from the Spui to Central Station. This monumental element gave the new Spuikwartier a strong backbone and with it Weeber in effect finished the work begun by Berlage. The labyrinth of alleyways through which the first *percements* had been projected around 1900, was at long last transformed into an orderly whole of urban streets and clearly defined lots.

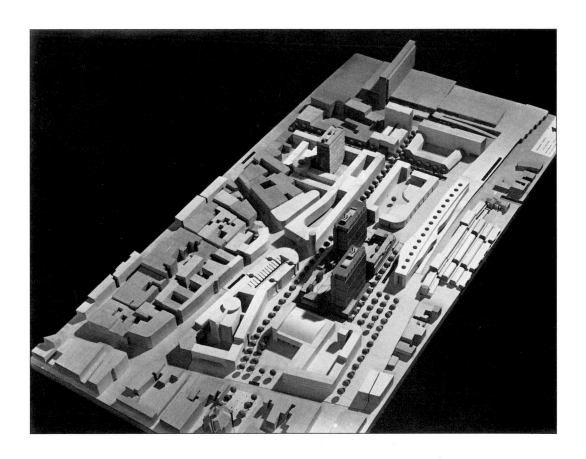

left: Carel Weeber, Development sketch for the Spuikwartier,
The Hague, 1977
top: Carel Weeber, Carel Weeber, Zoning plan, Spuikwartier,
The Hague, 1981

Urban Renewal

The 'Lavi-kavel'

Although the 1982 allocation plan had given a broad indication of the direction future planning should take it had not been concerned with the details, let alone actual building plans. In the event, several drastic changes in the building programme meant that the eventual development of the planning area was very different from that envisaged in the 1982 allocation plan. Weeber had tried to anticipate such changes by dividing the planning area into large building lots that could be developed fairly independently of one another, but a number of radical bureaucratic policy decisions upset even his predictions. First the Rijksgebouwendienst (Government Buildings Department) decided that instead of building the new Ministerie van Volkhuisvesting, Ruimtelijke Ordening en Milieu (Ministry for Housing, Spacial Planning and Environment, VROM) outside The Hague as originally planned, it would build it in the Spuikwartier on the two lots adjacent to Central Station.[1] Three years later in 1986, Duivesteijn forced through a decision to build a new city hall/public library complex on the other side of the planning area, on the lot bordered by the Spui, Kalvermarkt and Turfmarkt.

These two enormous building complexes saddled the Spuikwartier with an unforeseen increase in scale. But the final blow for the 1982 allocation plan came in 1987 when the Rijksgebouwendienst decided not to build the new Ministerie van Landbouw en Visserij (Ministry of Agriculture and Fisheries, LAVI) on the largest of the Spuikwartier lots, a wellnigh impossible building site fronting Zwarteweg and Turfmarkt on one side and tucked away behind existing development along Herengracht and Fluwelen Burgwal. Even the name of the site, 'Lavi-kavel' (LAVI lot), referred to the prospective occupant, while Hans Ruijssenaars's building plans, that he had worked on for years in consultation with Weeber, had just about reached the construction stage.[2] Although the decision not to build the new ministry was understandable in the light of the policy revolution that had taken place at the Rijksgebouwendienst, it seriously undermined Weeber's vision for the Spuikwartier.

The threatened deadlock was averted by a joint venture between the Algemeen Burgerlijk Pensioenfonds (State Employees' Pension Scheme), the Nederlandse Spoorwegen (Dutch Railways), the Rijksgebouwendienst and the city council. In the first instance these parties focused on the Spuikwartier and on

Aerial photograph, Lavi-kavel

1 Jan Rutten (ed.), *Het Ministerie van VROM*, Rotterdam 1993.
2 Frits Bless (ed.), *Hans Ruijssenaars architect*, Apeldoorn 1993, p. 98.

Central Station and the surrounding buildings. This area between the Babylon shopping plaza and the Nieuwe Kerk, originally dubbed the BANK area, was later rebaptized 'Nieuw Centrum' (New Centre).[3] Duivesteijn, whose architectural ambitions have already been referred to, took the initiative in the choice of a designer and came up with Sir Norman Foster. When it became apparent that there was no way the budget would run to this world star's fee, the choice fell on Rob Krier – a rather arbitrary choice it was muttered in professional circles, considering how different the work of these two architects is. Yet a glance at the competition design Foster produced in the late 1980s for the King's Cross Railway Lands, a derelict area of fifty hectares in the centre of London, shows that Foster is a much more versatile urban designer than the Dutch architectural world seems to imagine. Historicizing urbanism and high-tech architecture can co-exist quite harmoniously. The refusal to recognize the true, that is to say, eclectic, nature of contemporary architecture is typical of the parochialism of Dutch modernism.

Together with Krier, another, more retiring, leading character stepped onto the architectural stage, ready to play out the final act of the Spuikwartier drama. This was Ton Meijer, director of MAB Groep, a Hague-based firm that has developed multi-functional and usually complex urban projects in a number of European countries. Meijer's and MAB's familiarity with the practical aspects of architecture and urbanism was regarded by all the parties concerned as a guarantee that the complicated balance between the various social interests involved would be maintained. MAB, which was not commercially involved in the BANK project, was to act as an independent coordinator.

There were conflicting reactions to the initial presentation of Krier's vision of the BANK area in December 1988. Some were bewildered, the Welstandscommissie (Amenities Authority) was angry, but the usually hypercritical Hague architectural journal *Kridelahé* expressed qualified approval.[4] The confusion is scarcely surprising for Krier's design was unquestionably a very daring experiment, certainly within the unimaginative world of Dutch urbanism. The plan was extremely vague, not to say downright impracticable on countless points of detail. The observer was forced into a 'willing suspension of disbelief': first a decision of principle, then the details'. Those most directly concerned, the BANK partners, naturally had their own doubts about the design and it was no mean achievement on Meijer's part that he succeeded in keeping the peace between the designer and his clients.

Duivesteijn, during his years as alderman in The Hague, had invented the motto 'urban renewal through architectural design'. In a certain sense Weeber's plan for the Spuikwartier had likewise anticipated an architectural solution to the urbanistic problems in the centre of The Hague; Krier, however, went a step further. His vision of the BANK area was dominated by the tradition of civil art, with the result that architecture and all functional requirements were mercilessly subordinated to the outward appearance of the urban space. It was immediately clear that this approach would result in a long succession of thorny design problems, so the fact that part of Krier's plan for the BANK area is about to be realized is nothing short of an 'architectural miracle'.

Four years separated Krier's original BANK area scenario, dated June 1988, and the definitive master plan for the Lavi-kavel component of the BANK project, dated October 1992. It takes a minimum of three

3   *Den Haag Nieuw Centrum*, The Hague 1990 (Hague City
    Council publication).
4   Peter Drijver, 'Met Krier meer plezier?', in: *Kridelahé*, 3 (1989)
    no. 8, p. 3.

years to get a building to the construction stage; urban planning demands a good deal more patience. The BANK plan, seen by many from the outset as a crazy undertaking, underwent a series of changes whereby the original, rather over-ambitious, boundaries of the planning area gradually shrank to more realistic proportions. In June 1988 the plan covered the entire area between Babylon and the Nieuwe Kerk, later, in the 'Strategic BANK Plan', only the Lavi-kavel and the immediate vicinity of Central Station were involved and ultimately, when it came to structurally, functionally and financially realistic planning, only the Lavi-kavel remained.

In the early stages of the BANK plan the development plan for the Lavi-kavel evolved via an in-between step from a purely academic concept into a design in which it was possible to discern the broad outlines of the final master plan. In the first version of June 1988, a round plaza was projected in the centre of the planning area with streets fanning out in all directions. Apart from this extremely formal composition, the design was dominated by a large square that linked Kalvermarkt by a direct route to the side entrance of Central Station. Three side-streets connected the Turfmarkt route to the Kalvermarkt-Central Station route.

This proposal did not in fact solve the problem of the tram route between Kalvermarkt and Central Station. The projected large square might have been a fine example of urban space but there was no indication anywhere that it was also expected to serve as a tram yard. The projected side-streets providing a link with the Turfmarkt were problematical because it was unclear how they were to intersect with the elevated tram viaduct leading to the roof of Central Station. Although such practical details were probably not the important issue during this first stage of the design process – it was more concerned with producing a vision of the urban space – the BANK partners must nevertheless have had exceptional confidence in Krier's ability to deliver the goods.

In the long run their confidence would be rewarded, but the second version of this proposal, dated December 1988, was certainly no improvement on the first. The round plaza with its star-shaped street

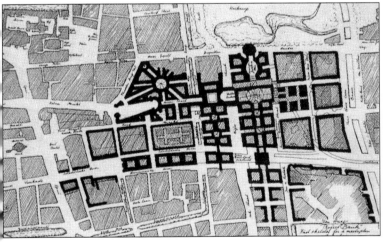

pattern had disappeared only to be replaced by an urban space that lacked definition, while two of the three streets leading off it went nowhere. The large square had become still larger but to dubious effect. The form of the square was now weaker and nothing could alter the fact that it was a glorified tram yard. One new feature in this version was the Transitorium, a seventy-metre-high office tower erected in the 1960s and evidently there to stay. Although the Transitorium had been a fixture in the plans drawn up by Weeber and Ruijssenaars, it had evidently been overlooked in Krier's original plan for the BANK area.

In both these early versions of the development proposal for the Lavi-kavel, the Kalvermarkt-Central Station link

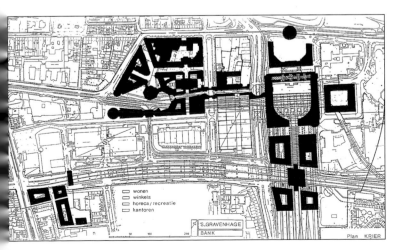

top: Rob Krier, BANK-area, with third route, June 1988
bottom: Rob Krier, BANK-area, with third route, December 1988

was a crucial programmatic element. Understandably, given that the BANK project's objective was to integrate Central Station and its environs with the urban fabric of the old town centre. Yet perhaps this 'third route', in addition to Herengracht and Turfmarkt, was a bit too much of a good thing from an urbanistic point of view. In any event, once the VROM building was on the drawing board, complete with a passageway focused on the Turfmarkt route and, at the city's insistence, incorporating retail space, the Rijksgebouwendienst lost interest in collaborating on the development of a – competing – third route. It made no bones about its loss of interest and this was reason enough Dutch Railways, perhaps understandably, to lose confidence in the BANK project.

In the third version of the development plan, dated June 1990, the third route was still visible but in a very rudimentary form, as if to say, 'I'm still here if you should change your mind'. Many of those involved still regret its passing but a closer look at this design, also known as the 'Strategic BANK Plan', makes one wonder whether, all things considered, the disappearance of the third route did not perhaps nudge the development plan in the right direction. Through routes do not suit Krier's urbanist ideas; he prefers introverted, restful urban spaces, streets that are more than the sum of their extremities.

With the disappearance of the third route, and with it the emphasis on a stream of people moving between Kalvermarkt and Central Station, the Lavi-kavel plan began to look a lot more static and evenly balanced. This gave Krier the opportunity to introduce a pet motif: the horseshoe-shaped square, an element that had also served as a node in the urban space in his reconstruction plan for Stuttgart (Österreichische Platz). Around this square, at the heart of the development area, things began to fall into place; it created a well-situated centre of gravity that had been lacking in previous versions. The link with Fluwelen Burgwal acquired a more or less permanent character, while the diagonal axis Herengracht-new square-Turfmarkt started to emerge. However, the building-over of the tram viaduct, between the square and the Turfmarkt, was still fairly vague and the integration of the Transitorium – especially on the scale-model – was frankly unconvincing.

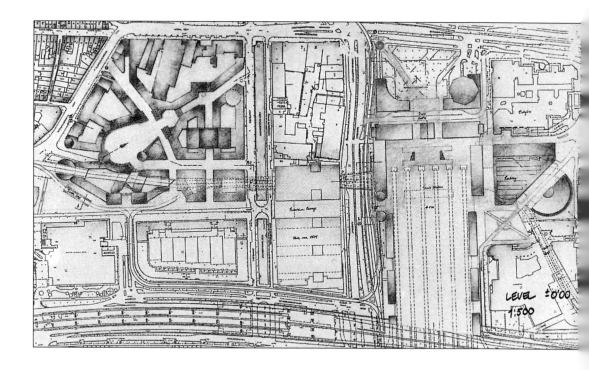

Fresh impetus

In June 1990 Krier's third development plan looked unlikely to survive. It was far from complete and the disappearance of the third route had left the BANK-project high and dry. At city hall Duivesteijn had been succeeded by Peter Noordanus while the Rijksgebouwendienst had a new government architect in the person of Kees Rijnboutt. At this critical moment, however, Noordanus and Rijnboutt wisely refrained from dismissing Krier. Instead, they came up with another solution that was to prove genuinely constructive. Rijnboutt organized a workshop in which Krier was to collaborate with several Dutch architects to try to turn the development plan for the Lavi-kavel into a workable proposition.

In many respects 1990 was the best year in decades for architecture in The Hague. It saw the launching of 'De Kern Gezond' (The Healthy Heart), an ambitious project aimed at refurbishing public space in the town centre, which was nominated for the government prize for building and housing, the Bronze Beaver, in 1992.[5] The city council also reacted promptly to the government's *Fourth Policy Document on Planning (Extra)* that had appeared in 1988, with a memorandum entitled 'The Hague, New Centre'. In fact The Hague in 1990 was beginning to reap the benefits of major policy changes set in train in the mid-1980s. It was then that Ed Nijpels, the youthful (Liberal) Minister of Housing, Spacial Planning and Environment had set out a more market-oriented course for Dutch urban development and for national government accommodation. This policy was spelt out in the *Fourth Policy Document* and in the 'Rijkshuisvestingsplan' (government office accommodation plan) also drawn up in 1988. At the same time the problems associated with growing road traffic were having an increasing impact on the siting of businesses employing large numbers of people. Urban centres, because they were well served by public transport, became spearheads of spatial-economic policy, which also opened up new opportunities for the centre of The Hague. To cap it all the (then) Ministry of Welfare, Health and Culture chose 1990 to publish its *Nota Architectuurbeleid* (Architectural Policy Memorandum) which made the pursuit of greater architectural and planning quality a matter of official policy.

Within a space of a few years urban development projects which had previously been unthinkable or at the very least unfeasible were now possible. Central government, the city council and the market finally succeeded in finding one another, thereby injecting new enthusiasm into the building industry. Krier's development plan for the Lavi-kavel became one of the first beneficiaries of the new mood. However, the step from policy memoranda to real decisions and action was not a simple one. No one knows that better than Rijnboutt, government architect from September 1989 to September 1995, and responsible for overseeing the Rijksgebouwendienst's radical change of course.[6] His own architectural circle treated him with particular derision, initially at least. The envisaged collaboration with the market, with investors and project developers, was regarded as a betrayal of architecture. A government building of any architectural significance, so the argument went, had by definition to be financed and developed by the Rijksgebouwendienst itself.

Such reasoning is based on the most peculiar prejudices and more particularly on a remarkable ignorance

Rob Krier, BANK-area, June 1990

5   *De Kern Gezond: plan voor de herinrichting van de openbare ruimte in de Haagse binnenstad*, 's-Gravenhage 1988 (Hague City Council publication). See also: *Archis*, 1988 no. 11 (special issue on public space); *Juryrapport De Bronzen Bever*, The Hague 1992 (published by the Rijksplanologische Dienst - the Government Planning Agency), pp. 28-31.
6   Kees Rijnboutt, *Mooi Nederland*, Amsterdam 1995.

of the history of architecture. To begin with, it is simply not true that in the so-called good old days the Rijksgebouwendienst confined itself to building monuments for Dutch architectural history.[7] On the contrary, the results were generally mediocre, while rumour has it that costs frequently exceeded the going price per square metre. It is an area that would repay more thorough research by critical architectural historians. The more worldly aspects of building have to date received scant attention in the history of architecture, a state of affairs that allows another myth of recent architectural history to live on unchallenged: the notion that project developers are interested only in producing lovelessly designed rubbish – the construction industry's equivalent of junk food – in collaboration with contractors whose contempt for pleasing architectural detail is if anything even greater.

Georgian London – a world-class monument of planning and architecture – was built by project developers. Nineteenth-century Paris was largely built by developers as was the greater part of the Amsterdamse Ring 20-40 (architecture of the interbellum period). In fact, collaboration between government and the free market is by far the best solution for such large-scale projects. 'In a free market economy', according to a Marxist study, 'speculator-developers perform a positive service. They promote an optimal timing of land-use change, ensure that the current value of land and housing reflects expected future returns, seek to organize externalities to enhance the value of their existing developments, and generally perform a coordinating and stabilizing function in the face of considerable market uncertainty. (...) Since the urbanization process relates to economic growth in general, the speculator-developer, who is, in effect, the promotor of urbanization, plays a vital role in promoting economic growth. Certain institutional supports are necessary, however, if this role is to be performed effectively.'[8]

Admittedly, this says nothing about the quality of the planning or the architecture but this too is an area where the developer and government have urgent need of one another. The developer is a professional originator who plays a crucial role in real estate investment; the modernized Rijksgebouwendienst is a major customer for office space; and urban planning policy is determined by municipal governments. Frans Evers, Director-General of the Rijksgebouwendienst, once remarked: 'If the politicians wanted us to build boxes, then boxes we would build.'[9] The same holds true for developers: if tenants prefer to rent cheap boxes, the slightly more expensive handsome buildings will remain empty and so boxes will be built instead. It is Dutch society that determines the quality of architecture and public space in the Netherlands.

The *Nota Architectuurbeleid* states that government has an obligation to discourage the building of cheap boxes in an inhospitable urban landscape, but it is a romantic illusion to think that a Rijksgebouwendienst that did its own designing and building would produce the desired level of quality. A short excursion past the government buildings to the north of Central Station in The Hague is enough to dispel this particular illusion, for handsome buildings lose all their charm in drab surroundings. It is the council's task to preserve the amenity of the urban space. This amenity, as is by now quite clear, is generated above all by a mixture of urban functions. Neither the council nor the Rijksgebouwendienst has the resources to develop large-scale, multi-functional projects in the city. Nor is this a task for bureaucratic organizations. Only the developer

7 Corjan van der Peet, Guido Steenmeijer (ed.), *De Rijksbouwmeesters*, Rotterdam 1995.
8 David Harvey, *The Urbanization of Capital*, Oxford 1985, pp. 67, 68.
9 Quoted by Kees Rijnboutt, in: Rob Stringa (ed.), *Rijkshuisvesting voor morgen 3. Verslag van een symposium 8 december 1992*, The Hague 1993, p. 10.

Rob Krier, Detail Master plan BANK-area, June 1990

can build dwellings as well as shops and offices, but that does not have to mean that the authorities are relegated to the sidelines, for they have ample opportunity to follow the process critically and if necessary to exert their influence before a building permit is issued or before a lease is signed.

The idea that the developer has an essential role to play in urban development was brand new in late 1990. So new in fact that even Rijnboutt, the new government architect, had not yet fully appreciated the ramifications of the new government accommodation policy. When he launched his workshop initiative aimed at finalizing the Lavi-kavel plan, he arranged for collaboration among architects and between architects and city council but he neglected to involve a developer in the planning process. Since then Rijnboutt has often made a point of admitting to this 'beginner's error'. This is no mere false modesty on the part of the person who, in the period 1990-1995, was responsible for overseeing a huge building programme involving close collaboration between councils, developers and the Rijksgebouwendienst. Indeed, Rijnboutt's repeated references to his beginner's error reflect the fact that he believes that collaboration with the market is the key to the department's new policy. It is interesting to note that the noisy criticism of collaboration with the market originally voiced in artistic circles had completely died away by the time Rijnboutt stepped down as government architect in September 1995.

The workshop

Despite Rijnboutt's beginner's error, the Lavi-kavel workshop held during February, March and April 1991, was a creative success.[10] Supervised by Noordanus and Rijnboutt, Krier and four Dutch architects set about fleshing out the development plan. The four Dutch architects were Gunnar Daan, Bert Dirrix, Peter Drijver and Sjoerd Soeters. They were expected to make critical and creative contributions that would show Krier precisely what can and can not be achieved in the Netherlands. The presence of Noordanus and Rijnboutt guaranteed a measure of administrative decision-making skill while officials from the city council and the Rijksgebouwendienst were ready to help solve any practical questions that might arise. Rob Krier was faced with the lonely task of defending an urban vision that was not yet fully understood in this cradle of modernist urban design. In Dutch architectural education the Holy City is still first and foremost a functional city.

Considering the interests that were at stake, the workshop can, without fear of exaggeration, be called a daring experiment. The safer option would undoubtedly have been to thank Krier cordially for his trouble and to ask some run-of-the-mill Dutch urban design firm to design something innocuous. Rijnboutt, who had studied under Van Eesteren at Delft, must have been only too well aware that Krier's design for the Lavi-kavel was extremely problematical. Narrow streets, curved building lines, perimeter blocks, a square: all urban spaces that modern urbanism had specifically rejected so as to save the architect from having to solve really complicated problems. And as if that were not enough, an ascending tram

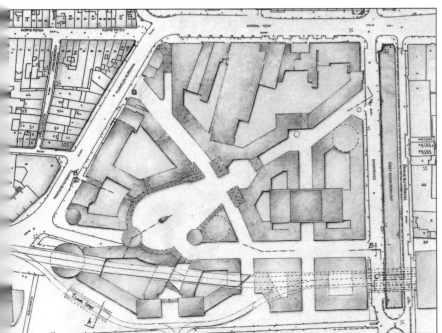

10 Rob Stringa, Peter Verschuren (ed.),
    Workshop Lavikavel, The Hague 1991.

viaduct that had to be hidden from view by being built over – subterranean rumblings could be heard as a whole army of modernists turned over in their graves.

The force field existing between Krier's vision and the prevailing views on city planning and architecture in the Netherlands did indeed spark off heated emotional discharges during the workshop. It is to the credit of all involved – for the outcome really does merit the title 'collective design' – that they succeeded in agreeing on a workable design which, if anything, shows Krier's urbanist views to even better advantage than his original plan. From some of the many drawings made during the workshop it is obvious that Krier had to put up quite a fight against heavy-handed attempts to trade his desire for variation and complexity in the urban space for optimum 'rationalization', in which the galleried flat, an undefined street level and the solitary office building pass for the highest wisdom.

After these initial skirmishes a climate of mutual understanding must gradually have evolved. Krier was able to defend his ideas passionately and persuasively and the pursuit of rationalization, as the above-mentioned drawings make clear, failed to improve the quality of the urban space. Krier's desire for optimum urban richness emerged unscathed, and the Dutch architects concentrated on the architectural problems that had to be solved if they were to reconcile modern-day building ordinances with the quirkiness of genuine urban space. The result was a process of collaboration between five architects, an alderman, a government architect and various officials, that would eventually lead to the sort of compromise that had been unthinkable in architecture since the days of Berlage: a compromise between the historic centre of The Hague and core-formation in the Spuikwartier.

The main physical change affecting the development plan was the orientation of the north-south axis. Taking its cue from the original idea of a third route to Central Station, between Turfmarkt and Herengracht, Krier's plan had from the outset been strongly oriented on Kalvermarkt. Even in his third version of June 1990 when the third route had already been scrapped, the link between the central square and Kalvermarkt remained a dominant element. This link was dropped during the workshop and the

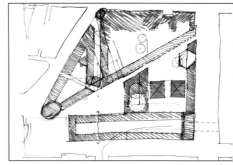

north-south axis became an almost straight line running from Zwarteweg over the centrally situated square to the southern tip of the lot, ending in another square-like space between the corner of Kalvermarkt and Fluwelen Burgwal on the one hand and Turfmarkt on the other. This was clearly a better solution. In addition to giving the pedestrian more freedom of choice it had the added virtue of greater clarity.

The improved link with Turfmarkt was very important because the technical feasibility of the three transverse links that Krier had drawn between Turfmarkt and the Lavi-kavel was compromised by the presence of the tram viaduct. Routing them underneath was impossible, over the top highly problematical. During the workshop two of these streets disappeared altogether; the third was drastically narrowed and it proved just possible to route it over the tram track via a six-metre-high flight of stairs. These interventions also had serious repercussions for the south-eastern section of Krier's plan. The north side of Turfmarkt had become an awfully long blank wall,

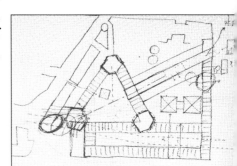

Drawings, Lavi-kavel workshop

although it could be argued that this resulted in a genuine urban shopping street where the infamous Zwarte Madonna (a controversial housing monolith designed by Weeber) might finally have come into its own.

The now-defunct third route had made way for an attractive sequence of squares, one an elongated rectangle, the other a fairly small circle, that connected Zwarteweg with the centrally situated square. However, the significance of this connection was rather ambiguous from an urbanistic point of view. The fact that both squares were to be covered over gave particular pause for thought, notwithstanding the architectural charm of the pointed hat Krier had designed for the circular square. Given that all the surrounding buildings were offices it looked very much as if a huge office complex – with two covered atria for internal circulation – was being created here, on behalf of the Rijksgebouwendienst. The plan notes confirm that both squares were indeed of a semi-public nature, meaning that after working hours they would simply be closed off. This, however, was contrary to the whole idea of public space. The Hague will never be able to achieve a

well-balanced urban development until the Rijksgebouwendienst finally desists from issuing such planning diktats. Huge government buildings should be part of the urban fabric; a building that shuts itself off from the outside world is nothing more than an obstacle in the city.

While further adjustments were thus being made to the relationship between form and function, the architects were also busy putting some flesh on the bare bones of Krier's schematic development plan. This was no easy task because whereas the development had an extremely complex form, modern planning regulations tend to presuppose a uniform regularity. Given the relatively short time available to the designers during the workshop, the result was surprisingly well-balanced and well thought-out; at some point the collaboration must have been highly creative. Once Krier had managed to make his intentions clear, the concept took on a dynamic character and the abstract notion of 'Stadtraum' began to acquire concrete form. The miracle Rijnboutt had envisaged did indeed occur: the workshop produced a design that none of the designers or other parties concerned could have come up with on their own. It was a phenomenon that the De Stijl fraternity had long ago dubbed a 'construction collective'. But the Lavi-kavel design process was destined to become even more 'collective'.

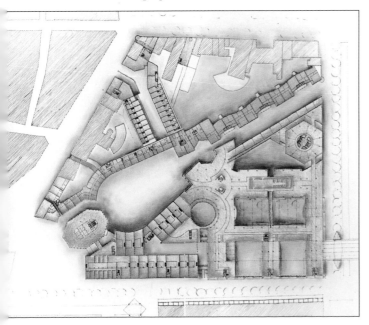

top: Model Lavi-kavel workshop
bottom: Zoning plan, Lavi-kavel workshop
offices
dwellings
other services

In the wake of the successful workshop there remained one practical problem: there was no developer involved in the project. This, as Rijnboutt has remarked, caused some delay. Once the project had been given the green light in January 1992, MAB Groep was brought in on the planning process. The choice of this firm was perhaps fairly logical considering the role it had played in the earlier BANK plan, but it was not chosen out of any sense of obligation. There were good reasons for deciding to work with MAB.

MAB Groep is a remarkable firm. There are so few employees that they all know one another, yet the project portfolio reveals a surprisingly large number of complex 'city centres': shopping centres combined with cultural functions, apartments and offices. The main secret of project development, it would seem, lies in efficient supervision of complicated design processes. Where possible, work is contracted out; MAB's own experts then cast a critical eye over the result, correcting it where necessary, and integrating it with other components of the design process to form a greater whole. One of their most celebrated projects in recent times was the Heuvel Galerie in Eindhoven, nominated for the Bronze Beaver award in 1992. This substantial project, which naturally involved collaboration with the city council, was described by the jury as 'a completely new centre, created in a fairly amorphous location'.[11] No small compliment when one realizes that this centre was hatched out in a rather grand villa on a fashionable residential street in The Hague.

In terms of the basic problem facing the designers, the Heuvel Galerie and the Lavi-kavel were not dissimilar: both involved creating new city centre functions in a complex urban situation. In terms of size, however, the Hague project was of an entirely different order: more like a city than a shopping complex in a provincial town. Moreover, the Heuvel Galerie was a single architectural entity, whereas the task in The Hague, in accordance with Krier's vision, was to turn a collection of different buildings into a varied but coherent whole. It was this sense of balance, for which no formula exists but which everybody is familiar with from historic streetscapes, that was the main objective of the design process. The urbanistic and archi-tectural ambitions were formidable and more to the point, experimental, for an urban development plan by Krier on this scale had never been realized before. The Hague city council, the Rijksgebouwendienst and MAB Groep were thus together entering upon a new chapter in the history of core-formation and urban renewal, a chapter first designated by its old name, Lavi-kavel, but later permanently rechristened The Resident.

In certain respects the prejudice architectural connoisseurs harbour against project developers is understandable. When all's said and done, nothing can beat art for art's sake – the perfect detail, the column capitals of Greek temples, flawlessly stacked to monumental heights, the meticulous joinery in a Frank Lloyd Wright house. The fact remains that nowadays real estate is a product that has to be traded and rented on the open market. Every prospective buyer or tenant wants luxury accommodation at knock-down prices and any architect worth his salt will try to turn the lowliest chicken coop into a cathedral. It is the

11 *Juryrapport De Bronzen Bever*, (see note 6), p. 23.

task of the (ambitious) developer to achieve the best possible balance between dream and reality. It is not so much that dreams are illusory, but rather that Wright's houses were very expensive indeed and the reality of a standard dwelling or a marketable square metre of office space is another reality altogether. Compared with their near neighbours, the Dutch pay lower rentals for both houses and offices. Real estate investors, however, still expect a reasonably high return and that means narrower margins for urban development and architecture.

Put another way: when a developer enters the scene, the market bares its teeth. MAB did not automatically accept the workshop's plan for the Lavi-kavel. Between February and October 1992 various parties worked on a modified version of the design. These included the architects who had taken part in the workshop as well as a variety of technical advisers, including the engineering consultants Grabowsky & Poort, who would later play an important role in working out the details of the plans. At this stage of the planning the project really started to come alive as a sense of reality set in. The Rijksgebouwendienst undertook to rent a large portion of the available office space on behalf of the (then) Ministry of Welfare, Health and Culture. Zürich Leven, a big player in international insurance, decided to establish its new Dutch headquarters in the office building near the Zwarteweg-Herengracht corner.

Although most of the changes made during this period were of a functional nature they were not without consequences for the form. Initially, it had been proposed to locate the dwelling function around the outside of the planning area. This proposal was based on Duivesteijn's ideal of, as he put it, 'intensifying the feeling of living in the city centre'.[12] A very understandable viewpoint given the dismal consequences of the almost wholesale depopulation of the inner cities that has been a feature of the twentieth century. But actually living in a city centre is not as easy as it sounds. People need a measure of peace and quiet, so from a functional point of view dwellings should be located as far as possible in peaceful surroundings.

All things considered, the functional permutations the plan underwent at this stage were only logical, given that the nature of the design had been substantially altered during the workshop. With the permanent disappearance of the third route, the Lavi-kavel had started to look like a self-contained piece of city grouped around a central square which, like all squares, was more an area of rest than a dynamic hub. Consciously or not, this area of rest acted as a magnet on the dwelling function which became more and more concentrated in the interior of the development plan, in the narrow streets and around the quiet inner courtyards that link up with the historic centre. The resulting environment is fairly rare for the centre of a city: an oasis of tranquillity, not in the wooded hills of the Veluwe or somewhere in the rural Achterhoek, but at walking distance from every imaginable urban amenity. Actually, not all the dwellings are so peacefully situated; for those who prefer a view of the hustle and bustle of city life there will be apartments on Fluwelen Burgwal and Turfmarkt.

The redistribution of functions had a positive effect on the clarity of the plan. The three slim tower blocks ranged along the Turfmarkt street wall were replaced by three distinctive office slabs, set at right angles to the Turfmarkt axis and receding in stages behind the building line. The result, seen in perspective, is fairly massive, an appropriate expression of the high concentration of office space to the east of the plan's diagonal

12 Interview with Adri Duivesteijn by V.T. van Rossem, 13 december 1993.

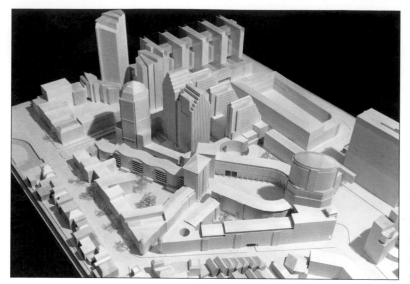

axis. It lends substance to the notion that the Lavi-kavel development should form a connecting element between the small-scale historic centre and the enormous government buildings around Central Station. The transition from historic to modern city proceeds by degrees. The urbanite sees the high-rise soar upwards, but always in an urban perspective, never in a modernist void. This urban planning 'knife' cuts both ways: it offers the possibility of achieving an uncommonly high density while at the same time generating fascinating cityscapes. Krier has called it the 'needle strategy', an allusion to the way church towers rise up out of the compact mass of buildings in historic cities.

The dwellings originally located south of the diagonal axis, on either side of the office towers marking this point and the entrance to the planning area, also had to make way for offices. In addition to functional motives, there were firm architectural arguments in favour of this design decision: the resulting larger office complex could be designed as a coherent architectural unit. This did away with the need – imposed by the Building Regulations – to stick dull, provincial balconies on a façade that should be making a metropolitan statement. This monumental Hague street corner has since been designed as a single entity: it is a virtually symmetrical ensemble that expresses, in an almost classical manner, a dramatic juncture in the city map. It was indeed the ideal architectural commission for Rob Krier: a building at a crossroads – figuratively, but also almost literally – of urbanism and architecture. Even Berlage, who once put this crossroads on the map, would have been happy with Krier's design, all the more so since he was of the opinion that genuine urbanism in The Hague was hampered by the 'diminutive scale' of the buildings in the court-capital.

Shifting the dwellings to the inside of the lot might have been an inspired idea, but it proved very troublesome to implement. The Building Regulations are extremely strict as regards the lighting and sunlighting of dwellings, but the proposed underground car park in the centre of The Resident, made it almost impossible to modify the buildings there so as to conform with the regulations. Moreover, anybody who has ever given more than five minutes' thought to a dwelling floor plan will appreciate that the combination of a circular and a horseshoe-shaped square is a configuration guaranteed to cause problems.

As already noted, MAB is in the habit of contracting out the design work and then checking the results. But it makes no sense to ask an architect to draw up a design for housing if the master plan is likely to fall foul of the Building Regulations. In order to avoid this happening, MAB had to do a lot of juggling within very narrow margins. Only now, four years later, as the building plans are nearing completion, is it possible

top: MAB Groep bv, Model of Lavi-kavel Master plan
bottom: MAB Groep bv, Lavi-kavel and the Master plan

    offices

    shops

    sheds / dwellings

    existing buildings

to see that their master plan was very nicely judged indeed. The car park, the dwelling floor plans and the Building Regulations are in total accord, with the result that the urban structure has also regained something of its historic complexity. All the knotty problems abolished by the functionalists have been meticulously unravelled here, thereby demonstrating that open-row housing – the galleried flat islanded in municipal greenery – may be the easiest, but is certainly not the only option for housing.

It was during this planning phase, in the summer of 1992, that a very different problem came to light. MAB was becoming increasingly disenchanted with the workshop architects' contributions. In a way this was understandable. The members of the workshop – particularly Krier – had naturally enough assumed that their urban design was the definitive plan. The commercially-motivated modifications that MAB considered desirable were consequently greeted with a decided lack of enthusiasm. Only Soeters seemed to appreciate that it was necessary to submit the design to further critical examination.

In the face of this impasse Ton Meijer became convinced that what was needed was a fresh injection of architectural creativity in the form of a few internationally famous architects. And so, after due consultation with Noordanus and Rijnboutt, the design team was augmented with Pelli, Graves and Natalini. The results, as Meijer had expected, were quite spectacular. Not only did each of these three designers produce a powerful design for The Resident, but their enthusiasm for the project as an architectural assignment served to stimulate the others. In particular the pleasure the two Americans took in the European context of the problem threw new light on Krier's efforts to restore to the urban space some of its original complexity, while their genuine interest in the Dutch architectural tradition had an inspirational effect on the Dutch architects, confronting them with architectural riches that are so taken for granted in the Netherlands that no one sees them any more.

The total number of dwellings was reduced slightly during the course of 1992 but this was mitigated by the fact that all the office space in the centre of the planning area had made way for housing. Both the towers on the diagonal axis, which act as boundary markers separating street and square spaces, acquired a dwelling function, while the buildings around the circular square were also ear-marked for housing. The latter entailed a change of character for the office complex on the eastern corner of the Lavi-kavel. It ceased to be one huge, closed unit around two covered atria and was instead broken down into separate units. This

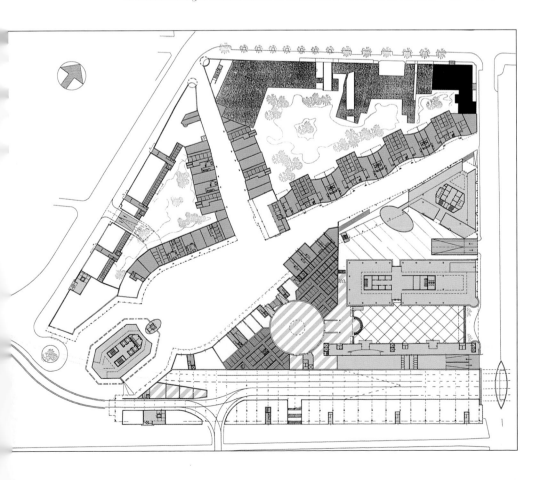

change was architecturally accentuated by the disappearance of the roofs over the two atria: they became more like public spaces, or at any rate, outdoor spaces.

These changes are a telling illustration of the divergent interests of the Rijksgebouwendienst and MAB. As mentioned above, the office complex concerned was intended to accommodate the Ministry of Welfare, Health and Culture. The employees of this ministry had and have a strong preference for the traditional government office: an autistic bastion in the urban fabric. However, there are limits to the demands the Rijksgebouwendienst can make when it is renting as opposed to building. The chances of finding a single client for so many square metres of office space are fairly remote, so MAB had to take into account that at some later date the complex might have to be leased to several different clients. In other words the buildings on either side of the rectangular square had to be so constructed that they could later be broken up into individual rentable units. This also made the idea of roofing in the square a non-starter: any suggestion that the square was the centre of one enormous office building had to be avoided and this should if possible also extend to the architectural appearance of the buildings around the square. In this particular case it was the government that was blind to public space.

In urban planning terms it would have been ideal if both the rectangular and circular squares could have formed an entirety within the public space, an outcome that would also have suited MAB, but the Rijks-gebouwendienst persisted in regarding the first of these squares as a semi-public component of the new ministerial building, in other words as a space that abruptly ceases to be public at the end of the afternoon. This was inconsistent with the principles behind the urban plan: the quality of the public space would be purely notional if this space ceased to be public.

Finally, there were two other important modifications that merit a mention. They concern the buildings along Fluwelen Burgwal where the original idea had been to convert a couple of distinctive older buildings to apartments – in particular the old Staatsdrukkerij (state printing office), a somewhat Berlagian-looking edifice built between 1906 and 1910, and its neighbour, the charming, historicizing building belonging to the Freemasons, built in 1845. MAB, however, opposed preservation on commercial grounds and so it was decided that they would be demolished after all. At a later stage of the planning process Krier protested fiercely against this decision arguing that: 'It is my task as far as possible to restore something of the historic urban fabric and now two attractive buildings are to be torn down – it's just not on.'

It always comes as something of a surprise to discover how cavalier the very people who make buildings can be when it comes to tearing them down. This applies not only to developers but also to many architects. Time and again they are convinced that the new will be better than the old. Technically speaking they may often be right, but in addition to its functional value a building, even an unlisted one, has a certain cultural-historical value. Everybody was a bit taken aback by Krier's vehemence – and it was at that point, when he felt that the issue was not being taken seriously, that he really

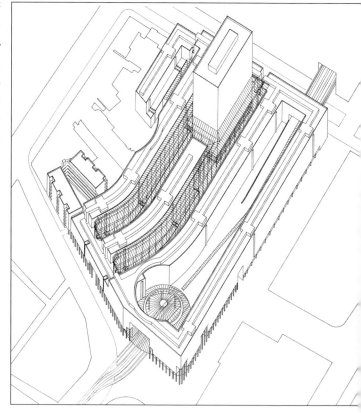

blew his top. In the end it was decided to try to see what could be done and Peter Drijver was given the difficult task of drawing up a conversion plan for both buildings. Since then an even better solution has been found for the Staatsdrukkerij; its new educational function fits in well with the existing spatial layout. The building where the Freemasons once pursued their arcane pastime is to be given over to offices.

The workshop design had also spared another building on Fluwelen Burgwal, near the corner with Herengracht. However, the planned redevelopment of the surrounding buildings left this corner looking architecturally bland, while retention of part of the corner development resulted in an awkward bend in the street connecting the central square and Fluwelen Burgwal. In this case the decision to go ahead and demolish can be defended with sound planning arguments. Not only did it remove an inconvenient kink in the short street, but with a slight change of direction, this street now headed straight for the Herengracht-Fluwelen Burgwal corner, from which point civil servants will in future be able to make a hasty beeline for the Tweede Kamer (parliament), via Korte Poten and Lange Poten. An important additional advantage is that the interior of the triangular building block between the square and Fluwelen Burgwal has become considerably more spacious, meaning more light, air and greenery for the future occupants.

Summing up, MAB's first contribution to the planning process, during the course of 1992, could be described as a cold shower – but one that came at just the right moment, on the afternoon of a hot summer's day. The concentration of dwellings in the centre of the design in particular was a key improvement, both functionally and aesthetically. It certainly made the Lavi-kavel a more attractive residential option, while the concentration of offices on the Central Station side made it possible to articulate the difference in scale between the old centre and the new city more clearly. The developer introduced a refreshing perspective. All the other modifications reveal a similar pattern: the old one-two between the city council and the Rijks-gebouwendienst has made way for a more complex social 'dance'. The fascinating thing about this process is that it was the public space that profited. Of course, the various partners all had their own interests to defend, yet although they did not always agree instantly when they sat down around the conference table, they all recognized that living and working in the city is only possible if the public space lends itself to human residence.

MAB's contribution to the planning process was practical as well as substantive. All part of a normal day's work for a developer you might say, yet it still has to be done. Krier's original plan was very much a dream, an urbanist ideal that was evidently considered viable at the time, not just by the designer but also by Ton Meijer. Rijnboutt's assessment provides an interesting footnote here; the design, he opined, 'could not be translated into the Dutch context, either as a plan or as a building task'.[13] The workshop's subsequent feat of translation was indeed of fundamental significance, but even then, as Rijnboutt himself has stressed, the building task still lacked clarity on a number of points. But by the time The Resident master plan was finally approved by the Committee of Council on 9 December 1992, it was urbanistically, functionally, financially and structurally a totally realistic project.

Before going on to describe how this plan developed after December 1992, it will be helpful to look at the approved master plan in a bit more detail. Its urbanistic qualities are thrown into relief by a comparison

Hans Ruijssenaars, Lavi-kavel design with the Ministry of Agriculture and Fisheries, 1985

with the 1982 allocation plan in which Weeber had projected an elongated volume that spanned the tram viaduct along Turfmarkt and closed off the southern edge of the lot. This was obviously a sound solution and although the block has since been shortened, this solution has otherwise remained pretty well intact. Weeber's plan for the remaining buildings in the lot, however, was unconvincing, amounting to little more than a diagram suggesting how to site a big ministerial building; it did not attempt to set up any logical relationship with the partially built north-western side of the lot.

Weeber, and after him Ruijssenaars, were hampered in their search for a satisfactory solution by the fact that the architectural brief for the Ministry of Agriculture and Fisheries building made it impossible to raise the question of the Lavi-kavel as an urban planning problem – it was, at this stage of the planning, quite simply an awkwardly shaped building site. Ruijssenaars's design was obviously better thought-out than Weeber's diagram but even in his proposal, with its slightly curved interior street parallel to the block on Turfmarkt, the Ministry of Agriculture and Fisheries looked as if it had strayed into a courtyard. This was partly the result of the attempt to incorporate the awkwardly sited Transitorium into the plan. Given such preconditions, the Lavi-kavel was a wellnigh insoluble conundrum.

Krier's plan was a perfect illustration of the fact that a good urbanistic idea can sometimes open up panoramic perspectives for a planning area the size of a postage stamp. Where at first there had seemed to be no room for a large ministerial building, Krier managed to conjure up enough space to design a medium-sized medieval town. He transformed the claustrophobic interior of the lot into public space, and with the benefit of his knowledge of historic town planning, he was able to find the perfect balance in size and scale between open and closed, thereby proving that even in a densely built urban area there is still a lot of space. The significance of this mental leap, which required talent and intuition as well as knowledge, can scarcely be exaggerated. The plan for the future development was still a veritable reservoir of problems of detail, of course, but at least the main idea was down on paper.

As described above, before the 'Strategic BANK Plan' was submitted for official approval, it underwent drastic changes during the workshop and as a result of MAB's contributions. Nonetheless, the underlying idea was clearly unchanged: the Lavi-kavel was to become a genuine urban fragment, an entity made up of smaller lots, streets and squares. Whereas the 'Strategic Plan' was a chunk of raw diamond, the master plan was a flawlessly polished urban planning jewel. The reality of many square metres of residential and office space undoubtedly had a sobering effect on this 'polishing' process. Krier felt that the pink building blocks

in his final version of the development plan merited an ideal type of development: four or five storeys, designed according to the principle of 'every house its own architect'. The intention was obvious: building blocks like the ones to be found in the Amsterdam canal zone.

Such an ideal, with its endless wealth of

13 Tracy Metz, 'Het werkterrein uitgebreid naar de stedebouw, een interview met Kees Rijnboutt', in: *Architectuur Lokaal*, 1995 no. 10, p. 6.

Rob Krier, corner Fluwelen Burgwal–Turfmarkt

functions and architectural vocabularies – in fact the cumulation of three centuries of living, working and building – is not, of course, something that can be built to order. Krier, who like all great architects is more interested in the ideal than in reality, has always claimed that the architectural units in the master plan are far too large. It is true that this has led to compromises being made between the buildings and the urban plan. The question is whether there is a ready alternative to Krier's admittedly very radical solution. A detailed study of the large building blocks of the 1920s and 1930s might well prove helpful in this context. In Amsterdam Krier has always been deeply impressed by the work of the Amsterdam School and it does not seem to bother him, or at least not too much, that there, too, whole streets and squares were designed by a single architect.[14]

Final model of 'The Resident'

14 Vincent van Rossem, 'Architectuur en stad in 1913: de overstap van bouwkunst naar stedebouw', in: Jan de Vries (ed.), *Nederland 1913. Een reconstructie van het culturele leven*, Amsterdam/Haarlem 1988, pp. 132-154.

An imaginary walk through the master plan reveals the following picture. At the southern tip of the diagonal axis, opposite the city hall and the Ministries of Foreign Affairs and Justice, rises an ensemble of office buildings: a tall ovoid tower flanked by two lower buildings. Between the tower and these two buildings are two streets leading to the central square. Krier's design for this ensemble sets the architectural tone for the entire project: plenty of variation with the tradition of brick as leitmotif. Continuing along Fluwelen Burgwal, the walker passes a series of different buildings. First part of Krier's office complex, followed by the Freemasons' building and the old Staatsdrukkerij, familiar façades which, contrary to the master plan, will not now be demolished. Only the Staatsdrukkerij's central entrance will disappear, to make way for the entrance to the large underground car park, a somewhat inelegant solution that has come in for criticism from the Welstandscommissie. Between the Staatsdrukkerij and the corner of Herengracht, there will be a block with dwellings and shops designed by Gunnar Daan, one of the workshop participants. In fact this project is in two sections, for near the Herengracht corner the outer wall is cut in two by a new side street leading to the central square and named after Calliope, the Muse of epic poetry. The irregular building lines in this street are intended to catch and hold the walker's eye before it can stray too hastily to the square further down. This urbanistic suggestion of a certain spatial intimacy, as of a picturesque little street, presented Thon Karelse, the architect of both street façades, with a tricky design problem. Manipulation of scale does not mesh well with the usual, to all intents and purposes strictly functional, approach to housing design in the Netherlands.

As the walker enters the square, a veritable kaleidoscope of perspectives opens up. Most observers will probably realize, either intuitively or after a little reflection, that this space actually functions like an urbanist magnet, holding a number of spectacular contrasts together. In the background, above the square frontages, a dramatic massif of office space soars skywards, but the scale of this development is subtly caught up in the perspectives offered by the square: this is what Krier means by 'needle strategy'. His own tower stands like an enormous polar marker on the square's axis, embraced by the two curved square façades. If the walker then turns around again and looks back, he or she sees the historic

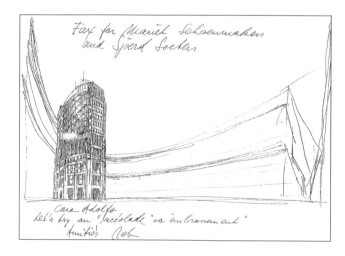

top: *Final model of 'The Resident'*
middle: *Rob Krier, Perspective of Muzenplein*
bottom: *Facsimile from Rob Krier to Adolfo Natalini*

Hague centre, a vast sky above a small-scale city, and the square, Muzenplein, which acts as both force field and mediator between old and new.

The development around the square was designed by the Italian architect Adolfo Natalini. Here, at the heart of the project, the emphasis is on housing; only on the east side of the square has some space been set aside for commercial activities, in the evident hope that some Grand Café establishment will provide the appropriate metropolitan atmosphere. It has often been argued that there should be more activity here, in other words, more shops and cafés, but this begs the question of whether it is pleasant to live above a busy shopping centre. Activity is all very well, but there is a lot to be said for peace and quiet too. On the northern side, where it narrows down and joins Muzenstraat, the square ends dramatically with two small residential tower blocks of different heights, also designed by Natalini. By ingeniously rotating both towers, Natalini has moreover succeeded in restoring an element of earlier design versions that had disappeared from the master plan: the hexagonal 'foyer', a spatial link between Muzenstraat and Muzenplein.

The walker who casts an eye down Muzenstraat will see a real urban street: narrow and with relatively tall buildings. On the right, the eastern side, stands the new headquarters of Zürich Insurance, including, on the corner of Zwarteweg, a very tall building with a dramatically shaped crown. This development was designed by the American architect Cesar Pelli and the high-rise section in particular, which dominates the Muzenstraat perspective and also determines how this future development will look from Herengracht, accentuates the north-eastern corner of the planning area in a virtuoso manner. On the other side of the street stands a long apartment block, a design by another workshop member, Bert Dirrix. These dwellings may seem a bit dark on the street side but in true urban fashion, the back of the block has a perfect south-west aspect and also faces onto a splendid inner courtyard. In functional terms, this large apartment building cannot be faulted, but in terms of architecture or, rather, urban planning, it turned out to be the problem child of the planning process and confirmation of Krier's criticism of large architectural units.

After this cursory inspection of Muzenstraat, and perhaps still a little bemused by the bewitching mixture

left: Rob Krier, Perspective of Muzenplein
right: Cesar Pelli, Artist's impression of the future development seen from the Herengracht, The Hague
bottom: Model Clioplein, The Hague

of Hague chic and late-modernist elegance that Pelli has added to the city, the walker continues his tour of Krier's masterpiece of urban design by crossing Muzenplein at the short side, to where a gateway opens in the eastern section of the square façade. A few steps here lead up to Clioplein where a pleasant surprise awaits those who are looking for an alternative to the typical Dutch 'doorzonwoning' (house with through living/dining room for maximum sunlighting). The name of this square, referring as it does to the Muse of history, is highly appropriate for this small, circular piazza surrounded by dwellings – it reminds one irresistibly of the historic city, of pre-suburbia days before the front and back garden with a sandbox for the children had been invented. It is another of Natalini's creations and as such forms an architectural whole with Muzenplein, but at the urban design level it forms a link between the quasi-traditional perimeter housing blocks linking up with the historic Hague on the west side of the plan, and the enormous office complex for the Rijksgebouwendienst on the corner of Zwarteweg and Turfmarkt.

This complex is reached via Parnassusplein, named after Mount Parnassus, haunt of the Muses, a long rectangular square between Zwarteweg and Clioplein. The complex consists of two separate and very different volumes. The northern volume is the old Transitorium, now a mere skeleton waiting for its 'face-lift' at the hands of the American architect Michael Graves. The volume opposite, designed by Sjoerd Soeters, is invisible on the master plan, at least on the ground level map. To understand it properly one needs to see it in cross-section, a perspective that also serves to point up the unusual character of Parnassusplein. As the drawing reveals, the lower part of the building consists of a gateway construction over the tram route, covered over with a car park. On top of this is a fairly large office complex, made up of three slabs at right angles to the Turfmarkt axis, with shops projected at ground level. The three office buildings by Pelli, Graves and Soeters are welded together by a continuous façade along Zwarteweg so that here, too, there is an impression of enclosure: the high-rise is part of the urban structure.

An unpleasant surprise awaits those who stroll along Parnassusplein to Zwarteweg and then turn right towards Turfmarkt. It is the tram viaduct, designed and built in an era when urban design had been reduced to a traffic diagram. The viaduct is just high enough to allow a car to pass under it but to the pedestrian, whose perceptions are rather different from those of the seated motorist, it seems much too low, unpleasantly low in fact. A few cosmetic tricks could help to mitigate this effect but the original mistake is irreparable. A bronze plaque in memory of F. Van der Sluys, former director of Dienst Stadsontwikkeling

top: Sjoerd Soeters, Design cross-section Turfmarkt–tram-tunnel–Parnassusplein
bottom: Final model of 'The Resident'

(Town Development Agency) would not be out of place here. After this barrier, the tour continues into Turfmarkt. Here the walker's field of vision is filled by the Zwarte Madonna, the Ministries of Foreign Affairs and Justice, and the new city hall, surely a remarkable piece of architectural history. In order to see the new, more urban street frontage along Turfmarkt, one must cross the street, for it is then that Krier's kaleidoscopic perspectives start to blend into one another.

On Turfmarkt, the three tall slabs of the office complex are succeeded by a much lower block of dwellings over shops, designed by Peter Drijver. This mirrors the scale of the Zwarte Madonna opposite and links up with Krier's office complex, the starting-point of the excursion. The relative complexity of Drijver's building, as revealed in the cross-section, is entirely due to the demands imposed by the tram route. The cost of such infrastructural folly is something the taxpayer would do better not to think about. The roofing-in of the Kalvermarkt-Central Station route offered an opportunity to create a roof garden on the inside of the block, which forms a link with Natalini's housing around Clioplein. Those who have no objection to climbing stairs can also experience the tram tunnel first hand by taking the pedestrian route through this block, from Turfmarkt to Clioplein: after a six-metre climb that brings the hardy pedestrian to the level of the roof garden a few steps descend to Clioplein. This public urban stairway, which is not unusual in hillier European cities, is bound to remain a one-off in the Netherlands. Drijver has had the presence of mind to give this element an urban accent, too, in the form of a slim mini-tower with a zinc cap.

Designing in consultation

Once the master plan had been completed and approved in late 1992, the second phase of the design process, the development of building projects, got under way, and it was here that MAB's coordinating role was to prove indispensable. The name Lavi-kavel disappeared for good and was replaced by 'The Resident'. As more and more people became involved in the design work it became increasingly necessary to mount a strong defence of the urban design principles underpinning the project. Despite the saying 'the more the merrier', the nine architects were seldom of one mind, and on top of this there was a veritable army of officials all demanding something different according to the government department they represented. In this whirlpool of visions, requirements and regulations Krier's original idea, to create a highly integrated piece of city, had to be explained time and time again to those involved: although the master plan was not an immutable given, already calculated down to the last centimetre, 'the spirit of the plan' was definitely the holy spirit of the project.

Guidance was available in the form of Krier's 'Lavi-kavel design guidelines', drawn up at the beginning of 1993. This document, containing instructions for the architects, was in fact a concise primer on civil art. If the Dutch urban renewal programme had followed these guidelines from the very beginning the result after twenty years would have been a good deal less inept, depressing and bleak than is now unfortunately the case. After explaining the ins and outs of the various urban spaces in The Resident, Krier went on to spell out the architectural consequences: brick should be used for the buildings, there should be no storage

areas adjacent to public space, no balconies overlooking public space, no experimental architecture, in fact the awful, quasi-socialist word 'housing' should be abolished to make way for a return to the dwelling as an architectural task. As far as the office towers were concerned, Krier cited pre-war Manhattan, the only place in the world where commercial high-rise succeeded in producing a monumental cityscape.

The task of the developer has already been defined here as 'searching for an optimum balance between dream and reality'. Not every architect begins with an architectural dream, but the very least that can be expected of a designer is a vision. In the case of The Resident one can indeed speak of a dream, for Krier's vision of renewed harmony between architecture and urban planning – the pursuit of civil art – was very much a dream. The first step on the road to an optimum balance had already been taken with the approval of the master plan. Not that this in itself turned the dream into reality – that is not how things work in the history of architecture – but the dream did transform reality, allowing a functional brief to acquire a new urban manifestation.

This confrontation between ideal and reality became even more tangible during the development of individual buildings. The architect, even more so than the urban designer, had to deal with a whole team of experts who examined and criticized his vision down to the smallest detail. This was MAB's task, and it was from the outset carried out in consultation with Grabowsky & Poort, the engineering firm responsible for working out the technical details of the architectural designs. Some architects, especially Natalini, wanted to do this themselves out of a quite understandable desire to keep the entire design in their own hands. However, with a building project as complex as The Resident, comprising nine different designs, such an approach, whereby all the details were drawn in a different way, would have resulted in chaos and would also have made it extremely difficult to organize and supervise the building process efficiently.

In addition to MAB and Grabowsky & Poort, the architects also had to deal, albeit usually indirectly, with various municipal bodies, like the Fire Brigade and the Welstandscommissie, each with their own particular requirements. The municipal power company, to name but one example, was interested solely in its own transformers, which are indispensable in a large building; architecture, unfortunately, is foreign territory to electrotechnical engineers. It sometimes seemed as if everything and everybody was conspiring to make a building and its surroundings as ugly as possible by coming up with the most impossible demands. In the first instance it was up to the architect to indicate when things had gone far enough. This was dubbed the 'basta limit' because at this point Natalini and Krier would thump the table and shout 'basta! basta! basta!' Yet the architect did not bear sole responsibility for the aesthetic quality of the design. The supervisor, Rob Krier, and his Dutch representative, Sjoerd Soeters, who monitored the architectural quality of the project as a whole in the context of the development plan, also kept an eye on questions of detail. Furthermore, the government architect was closely involved in the project,

Final model of 'The Resident'

not only because he was formally responsible for the ministerial building, but also because of his personal involvement with the history of The Resident.

All of this was going on more or less simultaneously. There were frequent consultations with the Welstandscommissie, which had some reservations about Krier's principles; the Hague fire brigade, which is a stickler for the rules, had to be consulted about the correct interpretation of the Building Regulations; and at a certain moment Noordanus had to go and speak to the energy company in order to put an end to the transformer troubles (a potent example of which can be seen behind Babylon). And of course a constant watch had to be kept on the budget, for architects are wont to forget that every square metre of rentable space is important, not to mention every parking space. Sometimes there were fierce differences of opinion between supervisors and architects, at other times the irritation smouldered below the surface like a peat fire. The idea of a 'construction collective' has already been referred to above, but the development of a project like The Resident requires input from literally dozens of people before the end result, in the shape of contract documents, is ready to laid on the table. And this is before the actual building process has even begun.

Very gradually, over the course of countless meetings, every nook and cranny, every bit of public space, every housing and office development began to take shape. At first it all seemed rather chaotic. A shifted column was suddenly found to have erased an underground parking slot, the solution to one problem affected and limited the solution to other problems. Occasionally this led to frustration, since the most obvious and logical idea, when viewed from another angle, was not always the right one. The housing specialist was confronted with what he regarded as unreasonable demands from the urban planner, while the architect was irked by the strict discipline imposed by the budget. There is no simple law by which the masterwork and the meter cupboard can meet one another half way, it is a dialectical process where synthesis is achieved through discussion. Step by step the stubborn reality takes shape, gradually a pattern appears in the chaos, and it is at this point that all involved begin to get the hang of things. Finally everything has a place and an exact size, the material has been chosen and the colour settled.

The nine architects involved in this design process have already been named. All in all it is a very heterogeneous group, although it is doubtful whether any collection of nine architects would form a homogeneous group. Probably not. To begin with there is a clear generational divide. Cesar Pelli, born in 1926, can be regarded as *primus inter pares* of the company, an architect whose experience, including with very large buildings, is so vast as to merit the old-fashioned title of 'master builder'.[15] His fellow-American Michael Graves is a little younger (born in 1934), and he, too has a lot of buildings to his name: the catalogue of his oeuvre runs to three thick volumes.[16] Although they employ very different vocabularies, both Pelli and Graves have an exceptionally acute intuition for the right form. The other two foreigners, Rob Krier and Adolfo Natalini, are almost contemporaries, born respectively in 1938 and 1941. They also have something else in common although it is not easy to define. Krier works in Vienna, Natalini in Florence: just like these two old European centres of culture, the two architects share a common tradition that is much less in evidence in north-western Europe.[17]

15 *Cesar Pelli. Buildings and Projects 1965-1990*, New York 1990.
16 Karen Vogel Wheeler (ed.), *Michael Graves. Buildings and Projects 1966-1981*, New York 1982; Karen Vogel Nichols (ed.), *Michael Graves. Buildings and Projects 1982-1989*, New York 1990; Karen Nichols, *Michael Graves. Buildings and Projects 1990-1994*, New York 1995.

Of the Dutch architects, only Gunnar Daan was born before the war, namely in 1939.[18] Daan has consciously chosen a different cultural horizon, that of the rural north, where Scandinavia is closer than Rome. The same might be said of the Netherlands as a whole but Daan is the only Dutch architect with a feeling for the atmosphere of the North Sea. Sjoerd Soeters is considerably younger – he was born in 1947 – and moreover a very different kind of architect, with a marked preference for strong colours and extravagant solutions.[19] His designs often come in for fierce criticism but his somewhat scatter-shot eclecticism has indubitably contributed to the destalinization of Dutch architecture. Thon Karelse, one year younger than Soeters, has been in partnership with Jurjen van der Meer since 1985. During its first ten years their office, Karelse Van der Meer Architecten has built up a fairly substantial oeuvre, notable for its quiet and restrained character.[20] Bert Dirrix (b. 1952) and Peter Drijver (b. 1954) are the youngest members of the group. Dirrix has built very little (perhaps because he is more interested in urban planning) but he did win the Prix de Rome in 1990.[21] Drijver, who runs the Hague office of Scala together with Mieke Bosse, has built a great deal and as editor of *Kridelahé* he has also contributed to the Hague architectural debate.[22]

On 5 October 1993, MAB organized a first joint meeting of everybody involved in The Resident. The architects had just started work and only Pelli's design was at a more advanced stage. As the opening speaker, Rijnboutt used the occasion to wax lyrical about the project's high aspirations, thus provoking Krier to grumble about the gulf between his ideal, especially the principle of 'every house its own architect', and reality. It was Pelli who raised the key issue at this meeting, by asking whether there should also be some sort of architectural consistency between the various designs. 'Of course', was Rijnboutt's response, not by means of rules, but by proper consultation and continual fine-tuning. Krier then remarked, although he may have meant it ironically, that a few sharp contrasts might not come amiss. Whatever his intentions, this was too much for Noordanus who stated that in view of the modest size of the project, order was an absolute must.

This debate about the architectural principles of civil art was to be carried on right to the end. It seems that Rijnboutt was fairly optimistic about the possibility of reaching consensus by consultation in a group of architects with widely divergent opinions and design methods. Rules would have made it considerably easier to achieve unity but the disadvantage of this approach is that it severely restricts the designers' options. The Amsterdam School had no official rules but every architect was well aware of what was required. At the level of urban design this produced a remarkable and often praised unity, although it could also be said that these residential areas suffer from a certain amount of monotony. Finding the right balance between rules and creative freedom is an exceptionally difficult problem when there is no basis of tradition to work from.

17 *Adolfo Natalini. Architetture raccontate*, Milan 1989; *Rob Krier. Architecture and Urban Design*, London 1993.
18 Bernard Colenbrander, *Gunnar Daan*, Rotterdam 1995.
19 Hans Ibelings, *Sjoerd Soeters*, Rotterdam 1996.
20 *Honderd maanden de Zwarte Hond. Karelse Van Der Meer Architecten*, Groningen, 1993.
21 Frank Wintermans (ed.), 'Bert Dirrix & Rein van Wylick', in: *Forum*, 37 (1994) no. 2.
22 There is no useful overview of Drijver's work as yet. Peter Drijver (ed.), *Pander en wonen. Geschiedenis van de verbouw van een Haagse meubelfabriek tot woon-werkgebouw*, The Hague 1989.

top: *Rob Krier, Perspective of Muzentoren, November 1993*
right: *Facsimile from Sjoerd Soeters to Thon Karelse*

During the course of November, discussions on the many practical issues got under way. These meetings usually took place at the offices of Grabowsky & Poort. In Natalini's project the dwelling floor plans were a constant source of worry. Contemporary building regulations rule out the type of dwelling that was common in the old-style perimeter block: no sunlight to speak of, no proper storage space and a virtual fire-trap because no thought had been given to possible escape routes. These sorts of problems were carefully gone through, step by step. Natalini, it soon appeared, had very definite ideas about the architectural expression of urban space but this was a problem for the supervisors to sort out. It is not so difficult to draw up a list of recurrent house construction problems. In fact, the functionalists did just that a long time ago. All such problems were finally resolved in the standard apartment building of the 1960s, the only trouble being that this brought with it the standard development plan and the notorious monotony of modern housing developments. As was only to be expected, all the old problems of the perimeter block reappeared in all their glory during the development of The Resident. It must be said that the Dutch architects often came up with ingenious solutions – clearly this is an area where Dutch architectural training excels. But the architectural appearance of these housing blocks often ran up against strong objections from the supervisors. It turned out to be extremely difficult to design the sort of intimate, small-scale façades wanted by Krier.

Almost the opposite process occurred during the development of Krier's plans for his office complex. The first sketches, as everybody had agreed back in November, were architecturally exciting. Particularly when seen in perspective, the offices gave the impression of a spectacular edifice that had nothing at all in common with the standard office tower. Yet even then, some reservations were voiced. It was easy to see that the façade, which was highly articulated and composed of a great many different elements, would run into difficulties with the budget. Moreover, it soon became clear that Krier had not yet given much thought to just how the design was to be executed. At this early meeting, on 19 November 1993, the atmosphere was still one of mutual good will, but when the demand to economize was more forcefully formulated, and Krier's unwillingness to do so became more and more apparent as the months passed, the situation finally reached crisis point in the spring of 1994.

The need to economize was not always so immediately evident as in Krier's case, and that may have made the disappointment all the keener. This happened to Daan and his project architect Haiko Meyer. Their design for dwellings and shops along Fluwelen Burgwal was initially greeted with unanimous approval. Despite the tricky problem posed by the Fluwelen Burgwal-Calliopestraat corner, the plans were lucid and the Fluwelen Burgwal frontage was decorous with a stylish accent provided by two rounded corners either side of Calliopestraat. Only after detailed calculations did it become clear that the plan was too expensive. For Daan, who was already uneasy in the midst of such a large 'construction collective', this was a painful moment.[23] Dirrix and Karelse also knew moments of frustration under the pressure of persistent criticism of their façade designs.

Like Daan, with whom he had worked for several years, Karelse felt that his freedom as a designer was being restricted. MAB's objective of marketable dwellings clashed with his preference for an uncon-

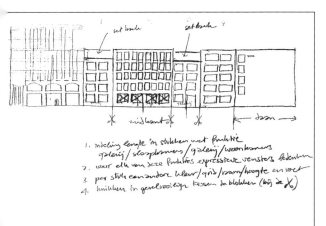

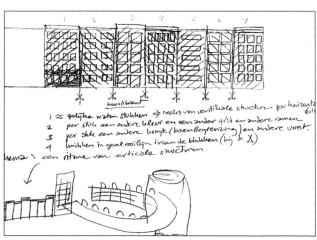

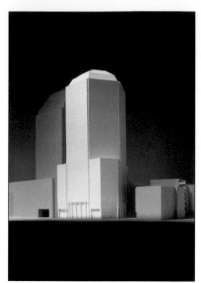

ventional dwelling type, and he felt that direct consultations between architect and contractor made it easier to be a bit more adventurous without incurring unacceptably high costs. But Karelse's main problem was with the urban design demand to falsify the scale of his façades to conform to the development plan. This led to a debate with the supervisors that was to drag on for months. Time and time again the architect received the same instructions, verbally or by fax: just make something that looks like a small-scale façade, and in the end he did so. Final judgement is of course reserved for the Muse of architectural history, but Rob Krier at least was delighted with the final plans for Calliope-straat.

In the midst of the many problems that started to crop up towards the end of 1993, Pelli and Graves seemed to be having no trouble at all conjuring up a perfect building. Both architects have a wealth of experience with large buildings, especially office buildings, so part of this seeming magic can be explained by routine. Perhaps it is precisely this finely honed routine for simplifying buildings that makes it possible for them to penetrate to the essence of the architectural design: the problem of form. Notwithstanding the functionalists' firm conviction, the endless talk about functional problems has yet to produce a beautiful building. The average office building has an entrance, preferably recognizable as such, and perhaps a relationship with the surrounding urban space, but for the rest it is simply a matter of repeating a standard plan a great many times.[24] Functional arguments can never help to find a way of achieving the wished-for architectural variation so long as the basic brief remains unchanged – and for a long time that brief has not changed much.[25] Pelli and Graves realized long ago that a big building – ironically a highly functional office machine – is a purely architectural problem.

By December 1993, Pelli, having started a little ahead of the others, had already completed a provisional design that needed little improvement. The photographs of the study models show how he solved the problem. The starting-point was, of course, the required volume, a massive block of square metres that needed shaping.

The essence was to make this volume as slender as possible: Dutch office towers are never very high and consequently have a tendency to squatness. The next step was to design an almost abstract white sculpture, without windows, colour or material but with a variety of possible tops. Then came the detailing, the colour and the material, in several different versions, after which a final choice was made. The source of inspiration here was Mondriaan's view of the West-

23 Colenbrander 1995 (see note 18), p. 107.
24 Ada Louise Huxtable, *The Tall Building Artistically Reconsidered*, Los Angeles/Oxford 1992.
25 Jürgen Joedicke, *Bürobauten*, Stuttgart 1959.

top: *Cesar Pelli, Design for office tower*
bottom: *Cesar Pelli, office tower study models*

kapelle lighthouse. Every imaginable option offered by the chosen solution was then subjected to careful scrutiny. The speed and apparent ease of this design process is mildly astonishing. The consistency of approach is further testimony to virtuosity; there is constant interaction between the detailing and the broad outlines of the design.

'Pelli', wrote the American critic Ada Louise Huxtable, 'consistently proves his case by designing some extraordinarily sensitive skyscraper skins. If he cannot make excessive size or bulk acceptable, he tries to ameliorate it by turning oversized towers into objects of precisely analyzed, remarkable refinement. His is a well-mannered artistry. He does not seek bombast; he divides, frames, and color-codes the thin, light, vitreous wall that is part of the modern technological miracle of skyscraper engineering, treating it as a taut, enveloping membrane or as a smooth aggregate of discreetly designed panels and subtly graded parts. As he moves farther away from "pure" modernism, he wraps his skins around the building in layers of glass and stone, like jackets, for an increasingly formal symmetry and sculptural form.'[26]

Graves's design for the transformation of the Transitorium – 'to redo the mass of this building' as he put it – was highly controversial, which is usually the case when architectural milestones are passed. A lot of people thought it was a ludicrous building and even when it had finally been approved, it appeared that the Welstandscommissie still thought it ludicrous. Graves is a radical anti-functionalist who denies that there is any need to express some kind of functional or structural 'logic' in a building's outward form. In his view this is all 'moralistic nonsense': his architecture is pure imagination, something that he makes demonstratively clear in his reworking of the Transitorium. In his hands the existing office building, a typical example of a plain structure with little or no additions, metamorphosed into a Dutch semi-detached, complete with two steep gables. In the original design idea these gables were rotated in relation to one another, but in the end Graves opted for the more restful effect produced by a parallel alignment of the two enormous saddle roofs. Any observer with a trace of functionalism in their veins immediately protests: impossible! But it *is* possible and anyone who knows anything about the Amsterdam canal façades also knows that an endless number of variations of this type of gable have been devised and built down the centuries. Nearly everything is possible and Graves has succeeded in recreating the very balance, albeit on a very different scale, that gives the historic Dutch house its special character.

This radical design also creates a fascinating architectural force field in the Spuikwartier. Just a stone's throw away stands the new city hall designed by Richard Meier, who was once, like Graves, a member of the New York Five. One would be hard put to come up with a more succinct summary of the architectural debate of the last three decades than these two buildings. Le Corbusier was the starting-point for both architects but while Meier has remained faithful to the modern tradition, Graves struck

26 Huxtable 1992 (see note 24), p. 85.

Michael Graves, Design for 'Transitorium' office building

out in a different direction in the mid-1970s. Shortly before this, in 1973, Graves, together with Krier and Natalini, had contributed to Rossi's historic exhibition in Milan which saw the inauguration of 'La Tendenza'. And here they were, exactly twenty years later, *bien étonné de se trouver ensemble dans Le Resident*. Natalini, too, had changed course in the intervening years; only Krier with his love of the historic city, has always been an anti-functionalist. It appears that Muzenplein has actually served to bring the three architects closer together. There are obvious differences – Natalini tends towards a classical serenity, Krier is more baroque and Graves makes it clear that even pop culture and Palladio are not incompatible – but the emphasis on the tradition of architecture imparts a surprising harmony.

The force field generated by Graves's building is fascinating not only for its architectural-historical resonance; in some curious way it also holds The Resident together. Despite the efforts of MAB, the supervisors and the Welstandscommissie to achieve a sense of unity, the various architectural components of The Resident are clearly distinguishable, and that of course was inevitable given the absence of any binding style concept, either in the Netherlands or elsewhere. A kind of unity has emerged nevertheless; it is a whole, albeit not a homogeneous whole, for the fault lines that appeared in architecture after the demise of the modern movement can also be detected in The Resident. Graves's design, which gives the highly misleading impression of being nothing more than a simple illusionist's trick, is actually so rich and many-faceted – American, traditional, postmodern and European – that it manages, by virtue of a sort of brilliant simultaneous translation, to avert a Babel-like confusion among nine very different architects. Civil art, it suddenly appears, is not just a matter of smoothing out, equalizing and imposing a vocabulary. There is also room for tension, contrast and contradiction, but this in turn makes even greater demands on the architecture in its attempt to turn an urban plan like Krier's into a symphonic whole, that is also a visual whole, a cityscape. In The Resident it is Graves who the precisely right tone for this endeavour.

While Pelli and Graves unerringly set to work in this way, Krier and Soeters encountered several problems with their projects. Krier knew right from the start exactly what he wanted but he became embroiled in a debate about the available budget. Soeter's problem was not the budget, about which he never complained, but finding the right form, and this proved to be a very big problem indeed. Designing a huge office building demands a very different sense of size and scale from that required for buildings of more normal dimensions. The task is in a certain sense more abstract because it entails a building volume that is beyond the normal human concept of what more or less constitutes a house. Furthermore, the brief in this case was exceptionally complex, requiring the articulation of very different building sections, without sacrificing an overall sense of coherence; the end result had to look like a single building. Even the most seasoned MAB staff members had to admit that it was a 'tough assignment'.

An analysis of Soeters's struggles with this design problem, which unfortunately cannot be explored in

top: Richard Meier, City Hall and Library, design: 1986-89, completed: 1995
right: General view of final model of 'The Resident'

sufficient breadth within the constraints of this brief history, is basically an exercise in thinking about architectural form. Soeters began with the idea that he had committed to paper when the three tower blocks disappeared from Turfmarkt, during the final development stage of the master plan in 1992. This idea, for three sharply receding office slabs at right angles to Turfmarkt, immediately introduced a tricky problem: what was the relationship between the three vertical high-rise slabs and the long horizontal façade along Turfmarkt? The clash between these two elements was particularly serious on the corner of Zwarteweg and Turfmarkt. Luckily there is a model that mercilessly reveals the nature of the dilemma: are the slabs standing firmly on the ground with the Turfmarkt façade slung between them, or is it the other way round and are the slabs balancing on the Turfmarkt façade?

At first Soeters tried to evade all these problems by choosing a different concept for his provisional design. The dominating and very expressively designed slabs were replaced by much less monumental aluminium boxes mounted on 'bridge heads' either side of the tram viaduct. This had the advantage of introducing a connecting element between the high-rise and the lower Turfmarkt façade, while the tram viaduct was also better articulated. Nevertheless, no one, with the exception of Soeters himself, was very happy with this solution. The Welstandscommissie regretted the substitution of vertical boxes for the set-back elements and MAB was decidedly unimpressed by the proposed solution for the Turfmarkt façade. It was suggested that this might, in typical Soeterian fashion, be too much of a good thing.

Despite the criticism, Soeters clung doggedly to this approach to the problem and throughout the first

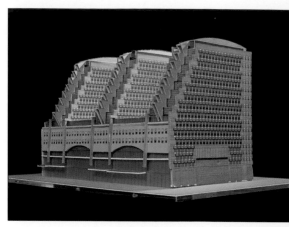

four months of 1994 he concentrated on finding a satisfactory solution for the Turfmarkt façade. Since the façades of modern buildings no longer actually have to support anything, this would seem to be a matter of mere cosmetics, but despite endless searching, Soeters never succeeded in finding a convincing compromise between the street frontage and the high rise. It remained, as the people at MAB rightly remarked, a rather messy whole. In the end it was Graves who suggested a way out by observing that it might be wise to do away with the curves in the Turfmarkt façade. This was on 18 February 1994. Soeters drew a radical conclusion from this suggestion, for as well as the curves he abandoned the whole idea of a continuous façade along the Turfmarkt. This changed the nature of the design idea fundamentally but although it was a step in the right direction, it was only the first of many changes.

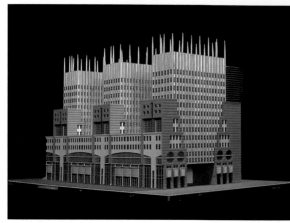

On 3 May Soeters presented a scale model that he had sweated over late into the previous evening. This model introduced an entirely new image for the Turfmarkt façade. The continuous façade element had made way for two façade sections that were obviously supported by the three office boxes. This was clearly a great improvement, so it is not so surprising that Soeters should have been under the impression that he was nearing the finishing line. He was in for a disappointment, however, because at the meeting on 3 May, where all those working on The Resident were present once again, his new concept was categorically rejected. It was Krier who put the bad news into words. We are all building in brick, went his argument, and now you come along with three huge aluminium boxes. Is that really necessary, how about a bit more brick? Graves agreed and suggested that Soeters try it out in brick.

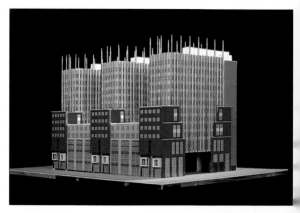

On 9 May Soeters informed the present writer by telephone that he had started again from scratch. By early June he was already discussing the new design informally with the Welstandscommissie and on 1 December his final design, together with that of Graves, was officially approved by this committee. On this occasion its members were even complimentary. And rightly so, for Soeters's final design may even turn out to be his first master-

top left: Albert Kahn, General Motors Building, Detroit, 1917-1923
middle: Sjoerd Soeters, Model I, II, III and IV

piece. The three slabs are now clearly 'grounded' and they are exceptionally finely articulated. The two façade panels are slightly recessed but nonetheless the Turfmarkt, as the perspective drawing reveals, will be getting a street frontage with a clear horizontal line. Another striking feature is the east façade into which the tram viaduct disappears: a comparison with the two earlier designs makes it clear that Soeterian expressionism, provided it is spot on, sometimes really is the best solution for an intractable architectural problem. In this instance one could even speak of a highly successful balance between Soeterian vocabulary and the typological character of the building. After two false starts a more or less classical American office building has emerged, comparable to Albert Kahn's General Motors Building in Detroit. Perhaps it is precisely this combination of typological serenity and architectural daring that leads to successful architecture.

Soeters's design has been examined here in some detail in order to show that not all architects are frustrated by the 'construction collective' process; indeed, Soeters surpassed himself. In this context it is also appropriate to mention Grabowsky & Poort. Architects who build abroad have to cope with unfamiliar building regulations and in many cases with the idiosyncrasies of the local construction industry. In order to produce a feasible design, therefore, foreign architects have no option but to rely on local expertise. 'Translating' drawings – which is what this comes down to – is every bit as difficult as translating literary works. Graves and his project architect, Gary Lapera, were extremely satisfied with Grabowsky & Poort's translation work ('they are very much on the team'); their experiences in Japan had been rather different. Further praise for the excellent level of cooperation with Grabowsky & Poort came from Pelli, during the final meeting of all those involved in The Resident, on 22 March 1995.

In early 1994, Krier's design was also going through a tense period and by April there was even something of a crisis atmosphere. Krier wanted to make a very extravagant building, while the aim was to create rentable office space. It was obvious that some sort of compromise was needed, and equally obvious that Krier was not about to make the first move. During a conference at MAB on 8 April it was decided to approach Krier with a suggestion for a compromise, since MAB was convinced that the problem could be solved. The hoped-for compromise was indeed reached soon afterwards, for on 21 April Krier came up with a design that met with everyone's approval. Krier, too, seemed to be happy with his new plan. Later on, in the car taking him to Schiphol airport, Krier grumbled a bit about the fact that he had had to make too many concessions. It is true that there are quite a lot of differences between the original perspective sketch and the final design of the office tower, but it is not clear what significance should be attached to this. Here, too, final judgement is reserved for the Muse of history.

top: Sjoerd Soeters, Perspective, Turfmarkt
bottom: Sjoerd Soeters, East façade, final model of 'The Resident'

Not every architectural dream can be perfectly realized; after all, Aldo van Eyck stayed away from the opening of his Orphanage in Amsterdam, because he was angry about the way the design had been executed, yet his building has gone down in architectural history as an undisputed top monument. Clio will decide.

Despite all the hot air about 'modernism without dogmas', Dutch architecture has always been very dogmatic when it comes to housing. And it was this bastion of functionalism that was difficult to fit into The Resident. The modern tradition, especially in housing, of building from the inside out, is based on the notion that the façade of a housing block is and should be nothing more than the vertical expression of the plan. The fact that the self-same façade sometimes also serves as a square or street wall is all too often ignored. The charm of this method is its uncompromising, methodical nature. The disadvantage of this unswerving logic, however, is that it leaves the designer little or no room for manoeuvre. If, say, the position of the meter cupboard is fixed, that is the end of any discussion about the building's outward appearance. Since there is no room for the manifestation of the urban space in this design process, house-building and civil art are almost mutually exclusive.

The term 'façade architecture' has been taboo in the Netherlands for over half a century. Now that the quality of housing, thanks partly to building regulations, can be almost taken for granted, and interest in architectural form in relation to urban space has clearly grown, the time would seem to be ripe to acknowledge that the façade of a building does indeed deserve a certain aesthetic autonomy. This means that architects should also be able to work the other way round: from the urban space to the meter cupboard. Natalini's contribution to The Resident demonstrates that this approach leads to the creation of a very high quality urban space. True, it has resulted in unusual floor plans but perhaps a modicum of variation in the midst of the plethora of *doorzonwoningen* should be seen as an asset. Natalini has shown in The Resident that a strong urban plan coupled with a strong sense of architectural form facilitates true civil art.

While the nine architectural designs were gradually taking shape, the problem of the public space was also being tackled. This exercise, however, was overwhelmed with good intentions, resulting in the curious spectacle of several different designers vying with one another to design the public space in The Resident. Alle Hosper was involved in designing the street level on behalf of a municipal project group known as 'De Kern Gezond' (The Healthy Heart). The Spanish architect Joan Busquets had been commissioned to draw up a design for the Turfmarkt route, between Rijnstraat and the Spui, while Frank Cardinaal and Richard Koek had been invited by MAB to design both the courtyards and the public space in The Resident. This was obviously too much of a good thing. Hosper in particular made no secret of his irritation with this overdose of design in the public domain. And he was perfectly right; there is only one public space.

After decades of neglect, public space was rediscovered as a task for designers in the late 1980s.[27] Unfortunately this revival of interest was not accompanied by the recognition that every form of excess is basically detrimental. The organization of public space should be as simple, as efficient and above all, as neutral as possible. Many present-day designers confuse this with bleakness and blandness. Yet old photographs of Amsterdam Zuid, taken when the district had just been completed, show that clinkers, freestone kerbing and simple paving stones can produce a very fine result. The decision to allow private cars to be parked free of charge in the public space was a fatal mistake. Since then the authorities have done their bit to finish off what was left with thousands of pointless traffic signs, anti-parking clutter, glass and paper containers, special tram lanes, dedicated cycle paths, speed ramps and pared-down maintenance.

The tendency to react to this state of woe with too much design and too many expensive materials is understandable, but this does not make it the right solution. It is ridiculous to want to make something special of every street. Municipal paving, provided that it is of good quality, can act as a restful background to the visual violence that is part and parcel of the city. Three designs for public space in and around The Resident is therefore two designs too many. It is a pity that Noordanus did not realize this early on, for a clear statement on his part might well have avoided a lot of pointless discussion. It was Alle Hosper, generally supported by Krier and Soeters, who finally managed to convince all the parties that a minimum of design in public space is already more than enough.

Along with all the differences of opinion about the colour of the paving and the question of which trees should be planted exactly where, there were of course some really serious issues. One of these concerned the function of Zwarteweg. In the historic city everything was small-scale, not just the buildings but also the flow of goods in and out of the city. However, the two huge office buildings that are due to be built on Zwarteweg are going to require mind-boggling quantities of supplies every day of the week. Apart from the comings and goings of dozens of lorries that this will entail, both buildings have underground car parks with an entrance on Zwarteweg. The tram viaduct is too low for lorries and turning is out of the question on Zwarteweg. This means building two extra bridges to reroute the traffic to Herengracht, and introducing one-way traffic on both sides of the water. On top of this, it was also considered desirable to erect a

Adolfo Natalini, Perspective, Muzenplein

27 *Archis*, 1988 no. 11 (special issue on public space).

diagonal pedestrian bridge connecting the main entrance of the new minister-ial building to the gateway leading to Central Station, between Turfmarkt and Rijnstraat.

The city council was not happy with all these new bridges and there were anxious mutterings about damage to the 'grachtenprofiel' (canal profile) al-though even the most seasoned guardian of historic cityscapes would be hard put to detect anything resembling a canal profile in The Hague. Cardinaal and Koek (C H & Partners) helpfully suggested taking a look at the situation from a different perspective by referring to Joze Plecnik's bridges in Ljubljana, where the water surface is also of secondary importance. The Oude Gracht in Utrecht likewise demonstrates that water does not always have to be the domi-nant feature of a canal profile; differences in height are at least as important. The two new bridges will undoubtedly be built, but by clinging to the canal profile idea the city council has failed to provide a persuasive, let alone strong, urbanistic concept for the new situation.[28]

The constant pressure to economize, particularly among municipal author-ities in the large cities, sometimes leads to mistakes that in retrospect turn out to be more costly than expensive public works. A glance at the Herenbrug from Zwarteweg shows that this is a bridge of enduring quality. A glance across the water in the other direction reveals how misplaced parsimony can turn out to be a costly error. It may not amount to a canal profile, but the water and the two embankments do constitute a valuable urban amenity. It is not so much the bridges as the cheap temporary solutions that mar the quality of this picture. The Herenbrug is a strong architectural element and as such it should form the starting-point of a new urban design concept, one in which the series of bridges, instead of having a disruptive effect would actually help to define the urban space. Plecnik understood this in Ljubljana earlier this century and Piet Kramer, in Amsterdam, understood it at least as well. But their bridges were certainly not cheap.

In the end Cardinaal and Koek produced a restrained design for public space in The Resident. The paving is for the most part done in traditional Dutch red-brown clinkers with only the occasional freestone accent for special locations. The source of inspiration here was the Binnenhof complex; a wise choice since it guarantees a refined form of tranquillity. Only Muzenplein has been given a festive touch, with narrow freestone strips creating a diagonal pattern of lines. These blue-grey lines also subtly enhance the spatial tension inherent in the shape of the square. Earlier proposals to accentuate the curve of the square with lines of paving leading to an imaginary centre, were always inferior in this respect. In the end it is the trees that will provide for a delicate, picturesque contrast in this otherwise relatively soberly designed square. A number of acacias are to be planted on the east side and these, and in time their delicate canopy of foliage, will serve to enhance the sunny side of Muzenplein – and perhaps of life.

For the various courtyards in The Resident, Cardinaal and Koek have aimed at a maximum of greenery. The possibilities for this, however, are by no means unlimited. Only the largest garden area, the inside of

Gerrit van der Veenstraat/Minervalaan, Amsterdam-Zuid, 1930s

28 *Probleemstelling Oostsingelsgracht-de Zwarteweg-de Oranjebuitensingel-de Resident-de Turfmarktroute*, The Hague January 1995 (internal Hague City Council memorandum, Dienst REO); Jörg Stabenow, *Joze Plecnik. Städtebau im Schatten der Moderne*, Braunschweig/Wiesbaden 1996.

the block bounded by Herengracht, Muzenstraat and Calliopestraat, offers a genuine opportunity to create a miniature city park complete with full-grown trees. It already boasts a mature beech tree which, will, with any luck, will survive the building process. In the considerably smaller garden between Muzenplein and Fluwelen Burgwal, the possibilities for planting trees is greatly reduced by the entrance to the underground car park, so this will be more in the nature of a large town garden. The courtyard between Turfmarkt and Muzenplein is in fact a roof garden – on top of the tram tunnel. The designers have therefore been forced to opt for a modest form of planting dominated by an elongated screen – if possible in the form of an artwork – against which climbing plants can unfurl their greenery. The areas between the high office buildings on the north-eastern side of The Resident are by nature problematical. Here the solution must be sought in the liveliness of the paving. Only Parnassusplein offers the possibility of planting a few very slender trees.

Regrettably, little has been written about the importance of greenery for the quality of public space. There is a lovely remark by Berlage who, while looking at the Canal Grande in Venice, noted that in spite of the architectural grandeur of the Italian palazzi, it was the trees that caught his attention, making him long for the Herengracht in Amsterdam. Happily, the Hague's Herengracht can also boast some splendid trees that serve to demonstrate what a canopy of leaves can do for the urban space. Trees are also planned for Fluwelen Burgwal and Turfmarkt. With a bit of fantasy one can imagine the future inhabitants of The Resident taking a stroll on a summer evening. Once around the block, or perhaps even a turn around the Hofvijver, a glass of wine under the acacias on Muzenplein. Urban greenery is by definition scarce but then every tree counts, every detail is important. Even a single tree, like the beech on Clioplein, can be a little oasis in the desert.

In the course of this discussion of The Resident there have been several references to Amsterdam Zuid and to the coherence between architecture and town planning so characteristic of the Amsterdam School. It is an almost inevitable comparison because Amsterdam in the 1920s and 1930s was the scene of a unique form of teamwork involving government, commissioning bodies and architects. The government was the dominant member of the team; the Schoonheidscommissie (precursor of the Welstandscommissie) had a very strong mandate to force architects to build in the Amsterdam School style, although this was usually unnecessary because the committee had already issued a more or less binding recommendation regarding the choice of architect. The public space, which included street furniture, transformer kiosks, bridges, and of course public buildings, in particular many school buildings, was designed by the Dienst der Publieke Werken (public works department), and it too employed the vocabulary of the Amsterdam School. The result was a perfectly integrated cityscape.

It is doubtful whether such a method could ever be repeated. Of course, one can never exclude the possibility that the government may some day strengthen its grip on public space, but it is most unlikely that architects' work will ever again be subsumed in a single style concept in such a uncompromising way.

Some time ago now the art historian Bernard Colenbrander ventured a tentative evaluation of the architecture produced during Rijnboutt's tenure as Rijksbouwmeester. 'There is something amiss', he concluded, 'however praiseworthy the huge number of

top: Herenbrug seen from Zwarteweg, The Hague, 1996
bottom: Zwarte Madonna seen from Zwarteweg, tramviaduct, 1996

taxation offices, law courts, prisons and other structures amenable to standardization that passed across Rijnboutt's desk may be. What is lacking is a thoroughgoing architectural standard, one that can be seen to recur in a series of buildings, over a longer period of time, if possible involving different architects working in a comparable manner.'[29] Colenbrander nevertheless understands that Rijnboutt, whether or not with a clear conscience, is no more than an accessory: Dutch architecture is currently dominated by an aversion to 'off-the-peg' architecture – every building must be a unique masterpiece.

A 'thoroughgoing architectural standard' such as Colenbrander calls for, can only arise within the framework of a tradition, when different generations work on a building task and in so doing gradually refine a vocabulary until harmonious cityscapes emerge almost of their own accord. Since the modernists' root and branch eradication of tradition there is little likelihood of architects developing any sympathy for the subtleties of historical architecture in the foreseeable future. So it is necessary to look for some other solution, one that will by definition be a stopgap solution. The history of The Resident provides a general idea of the possibilities. The architects were carefully selected and, thanks partly to Rob Krier's guidelines, a broad coherence was achieved. Whether still greater coherence in architectural vocabulary should be demanded is a moot point. As already noted above, contemporary architects are simply not very interested in stylistic unity and they are unlikely to respond favourably to any attempt to enforce it. In The Resident a great deal of attention was paid to the choice of material. Krier's guidelines opted for brick as the preferred material but brick, of course, comes in all shapes, sizes and colours. On more than one occasion the choice of brick was the subject of extensive consultations. One thing that had to be kept in mind was that a large wall area in a particular brick always looks different from the supplier's sample. All too often, Graves recalled, it was a bitter disappointment. Krier, who had originally opted for a red-brown brick quickly changed his mind when shown a building in The Hague with a whole wall done in this brick. He then settled on a very dark, almost black brick which turned out to be rather expensive. Fortunately this problem was not insurmountable for as the scale model shows, this choice of brick will give the Muzentoren a genuinely monumental character.

The concept of civil art dates from the period between 1890 and 1925 when the last heroic attempt was made to rescue something of an old European civilization from the all-conquering Industrial Revolution. The demise of civil art in the Netherlands can be precisely dated. The last attempt to produce a major design using the resources of civil art, was W.G. Witteveen's reconstruction plan for Rotterdam (1941-1944). Unlike the later Basisplan of 1946, this was no two-dimensional allocation plan but a spatial composition of street and square walls where architecture played an essential role.[30] It soon became apparent that the relationship between architecture and town planning was going to lead to immense design problems. J.J.P. Oud and Witteveen could not agree about the development on Hofplein and this served to convince the bureaucrats that Witteveen's principles would give rise to time-consuming debate.[31] It was C.H. van der Leeuw, who had already made architectural history as the initiator of the Van Nelle Factory, who finally cut the knot. He opted for a fundamental separation between town planning and architecture and in January 1944 Witteveen departed the scene – and with him civil art in the Netherlands.[32]

29 Bernard Colenbrander, 'Antwoorden op schaarste en verhuisdrift', in: Stringa (ed.) 1993 (see note 9), pp. 34, 35.

The Resident can be seen as an attempt to breathe new life into civil art. The design problems that arose here are in many respects reminiscent of the conflict between Oud and Witteveen. What was lacking then and is still lacking today, is a natural harmony between buildings and urban space. During the final gathering of The Resident veterans it was Krier who, anticipating the criticism he fully expected, spoke of an 'architectural fairground'. This verdict was indeed delivered not long afterwards by Hans van Dijk.[33] A final verdict must of course await the completion of The Resident, but the result may well surprise Krier. Given the use of brick throughout and a degree of uniformity in the final building plans, it is likely that a greater coherence will emerge than the individual designs or even the scale model might now suggest. Nonetheless, there will also be differences. Not even the most gifted designer nor the most ambitious developer can escape the imprint of history. In the twentieth century fin-de-siècle international architecture is dominated by eclecticism. Yet this can also be seen in a positive light. As J. Mordaunt Crook writes: 'The hybridity of Post-Modernism is merely an index of the heterogeneity of modern communities. Total styles are the product of simple societies or totalitarian regimes. Eclecticism – not necessarily historical in form – is the vernacular of the sophisticates, the language of freedom.'[34]

30 Cor Wagenaar, *Welvaartsstad in wording. De Wederopbouw van Rotterdam 1940-1952*, Rotterdam 1992, p. 146.
31 Op. cit. p. 195 ff.
32 Op. cit. p. 219.
33 Hans van Dijk, 'Den Haag vandaag', in: *Archis* 1994 no. 9, pp. 69-80.
34 J. Mordaunt Crook, *The Dilemma of Style*, London 1987, p. 270.

Project Documentation

Gunnar Daan

Bert Dirrix

Peter Drijver

Michael Graves

Karelse Van der Meer Architecten

Rob Krier

Adolfo Natalini

Cesar Pelli

Sjoerd Soeters

CH & Partners

Gunnar Daan

26 apartments
570 square metres of retail space
Fluwelen Burgwal–Calliopestraat

Gunnar Daan is an architect of long standing. He was also fortunate in that his architectural studies in Delft coincided with an ideological lull. The old debate between the Delft School and Nieuwe Zakelijkheid (New Objectivity) was over and the new puppet show featuring Aldo van Eyck and Carel Weeber, had yet to begin. Daan profited from this situation by developing a calm, somewhat craftsmanlike approach to his profession. By subsequently choosing to work almost exclusively in the northern reaches of the Netherlands, Daan was able to pursue this approach at his own pace until the Dutch architectural world suddenly discovered that it had an exceptional talent in its midst.

The *Architecture Yearbook 1990-1991* records Daan with two stylistically disparate works. While the notary's office in Leeuwarden meshes seamlessly with a row of nineteenth-century single-family dwellings, the other design, a harbour office in Groningen, is modern in a distinctively contemporary manner. This stylistic versatility notwithstanding, the designs have at least one thing in common: upon closer consideration it is the unerring precision of their execution that is most striking.

This is certainly true of the shops and apartments Daan has designed for The Resident. Stylistically they are not easy to pin down. There are affinities with the nineteenth-century building block which, given the design brief, is wholly appropriate. The two rounded corners of Calliopestraat are even vaguely reminiscent of Parisian turn-of-the-century blocks. Yet this feature also has a functional aspect, for the floor plans show that the future occupants will be getting a spectacular living room. The choice of windows reminiscent rather of Perret than of Le Corbusier is also indicative of a certain leaning towards tradition. Another remarkable detail of the composition is the blank surface in the Herengracht façade: although it too is implicit in the ground plan, it is also a potent example of historicism in the form of a virtually forgotten nineteenth-century motif.

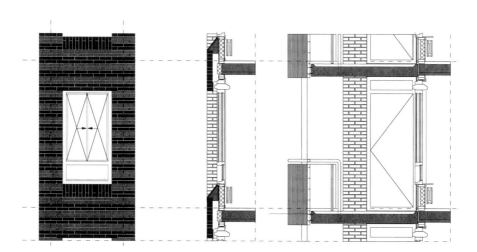

In this medley of half-forgotten architectural idioms from the previous century, the presence of Daan's hand is unmistakable. The design reflects his attempt to strike a balance between nineteenth-century excess, the cradle of the modern building block, and the austerity J.J.P. Oud introduced to social housing in Rotterdam as a prelude to the Functionalists' open row housing. Daan has worked hard to achieve a harmonious balance between the composition of the façades and the organization of the floor plans. His meticulous approach to designing is also evident in the detailing. Although Daan's Fluwelen Burgwal–Herengracht corner is more modern and large scale, it is not without a certain urban elegance.

top right: façade Fluwelen Burgwal
bottom right: back façade Fluwelen Burgwal

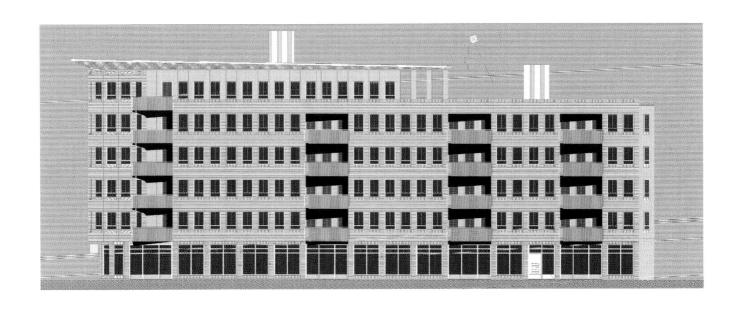

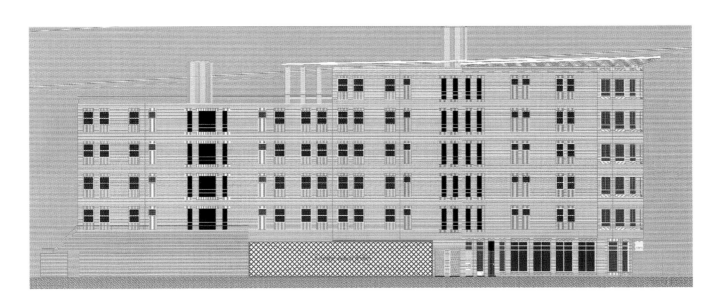

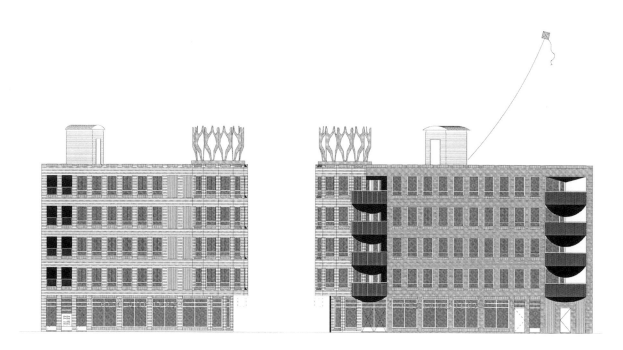

top left: façade Herengracht and facade Calliopestraat
top right: floor plan
bottom: ground floor plan

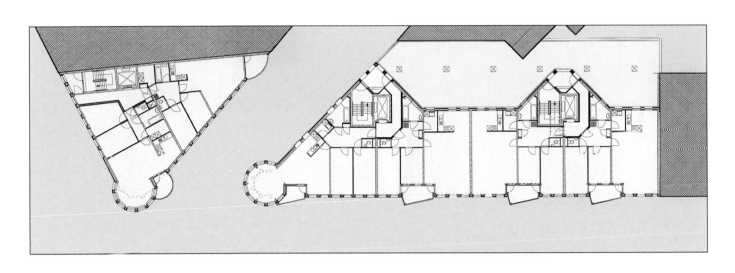

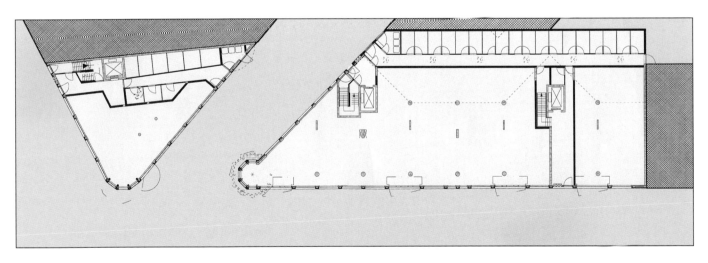

Bert Dirrix

40 apartments
1,560 square metres of office space
Muzenstraat

    Bert Dirrix was one of the rising talents (he had recently won the Prix de Rome) the government architect chose to let loose on Rob Krier's urban design plan. Unfortunately no detailed records were kept of the workshop proceedings but the drawings and the participants' anecdotes suggest a fairly tough confrontation between two very different design approaches. Krier views the urban space as the essence of the architectural task and expects both the floor plan and the outward appearance of a building to be subordinated to this fact. Dutch architectural training on the other hand has always been strongly oriented towards the rationalization of the design brief, whereby the structure and the floor plan are regarded as the most important problems.

    It is a minor miracle that the workshop participants finally managed work out a joint strategy, although this did not in itself solve all the problems. Because Krier also acted as supervisor of the design phase, there were many instances when Krier's civic art clashed with the rationalist approach of the Dutch architects. Dirrix in particular, whose working method resembles a search for mathematical perfection, came in for quite a lot of criticism from Krier.

    Krier is probably still convinced that Dirrix rationalizes his buildings to death in the course of the design process, but in the end he gave the large apartment building and the adjacent, lower office section his blessing. Dirrix, so it seems, was right to look for inspiration to Perret, in particular to his famous Parisian apartment building in the Rue Franklin built in 1903. In fact there are few tangible similarities between this building and Dirrix's design for The Resident. The point is that Perret, a confirmed rationalist, also sought a compromise with nineteenth-century tradition. Even later on, when his housing blocks had in fact become free-standing blocks of flats, they still recalled the urbane classicism of Haussmann.

top left: A. Perret, apartment building Rue Franklin, Paris 1903

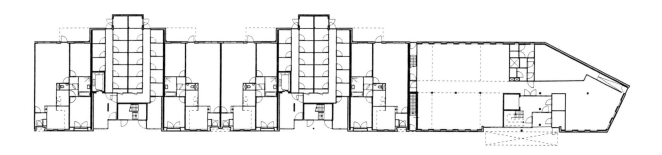

Dirrix's floor plans are actually much better than Perret's and the only point of similarity with the building in Rue Franklin is the sculptural articulation of the Muzenstraat façade which has the merit of letting more air into the narrow street while at the same time generating a rhythmical articulation of the street space. Future residents will probably be more interested in the access to and the layout of their dwelling. Although they may never be aware of the perfect mathematical order of the block as a whole, no one can fail to notice the building's generous design. Even those who decide to take the stairs instead of the lift will not regret their impulse. There are wonderfully large living rooms that get the morning sun at breakfast time and the afternoon sun in time for evening drinks. The balconies at the back of the building, which catch the noonday sun, look out over the magnificent 'Herengracht garden' designed by CH & Partners. It all adds up to a superior quality of urban living that is all too rarely achieved. On closer inspection, Dirrix's rather severe-looking design turns out to be an exceptionally pleasant housing block.

top left: floor plan, bottom left: groud floor plan
top right: façade Muzenstraat
bottom right: back façade Muzenstraat

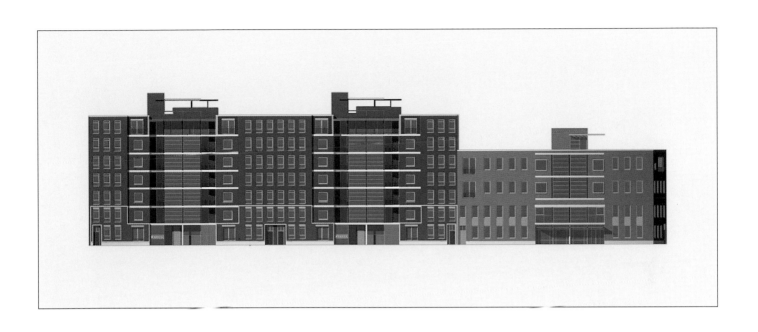

Peter Drijver

48 apartments, 680 square metres of retail space
Turfmarkt

Car park entrance, Fluwelen Burgwal

Conversion of freemasons' lodge, Fluwelen Burgwal

Peter Drijver, like Dirrix, was one of the new talents in the workshop. However, because his experience was largely in the field of urban renewal, his background and approach to architecture were very different. The renovation of the Pander works in The Hague during the 1980s, which involved converting a huge factory complex into a housing block in consultation with squatters, had already brought Drijver into contact with Rob Krier's ideas. The preservation operation was not confined to the factory building but also extended to the cluttered and hence charming character of the surrounding urban space, an ideal context for Krier's urban design ideas. When Krier started work in The Hague, Drijver had an opportunity to study the practical application of civic art at close quarters.

Drijver was an obvious choice of designer for the project to convert the old Staatsdrukkerij building on Fluwelen Burgwal to apartments. In the event the conversion did not go ahead for at the eleventh hour the building was given an educational function. All that remained of this commission was the difficult task of creating an entrance to The Resident's underground car park through the building's façade. The solution reached after lengthy discussions with the Welstandscommissie is both logical and elegant. Drijver clearly had no desire to conceal the assault on the Staatsdrukkerij: it is quite obvious that a hole has been cut in the street frontage for the benefit of the inevitable 'automobility' of the modern city dweller. Nonetheless, the entrance way has been meticulously designed as a stylishly detailed vestibule to the concrete underground world of stationary metal. The design is not without a certain irony.

In compensation for this much-reduced commission, Drijver was subsequently offered the chance to design a block of apartments and shops on Turfmarkt. The block is partly on top of and partly adjacent to the tram tunnel and the consequences of this siting are reflected in the plans and the cross-section. Further-

more, the block is intersected by the pedestrian route running over the tram tunnel (via a substantial flight of steps) to Clioplein.

Drijver found the broad outlines for the architectural form of the block by allowing this complex urbanist brief to be clearly expressed in the design. Here, too, a huge hole has been driven through the façade, in this instance for the tram. On one side of this gap is a tower containing the stairwell and lift and next to it is the public stairway leading to Clioplein. With so many highly expressive features, Drijver was able to make do with a very simple façade composition. One way or another the design is stylistically reminiscent of the 1950s, in particular the balcony railings which are only one cut above cheap fences.

Finally, Drijver also produced a reconstruction plan for the freemasons' lodge on Fluwelen Burgwal. The original idea was to convert this building into four exclusive apartments. However, this design, too, has been shelved because the building has a rosier future as offices.

top right: first floor, entresol and ground floor
middle right: façade Turfmarkt
bottom right: back façade Turfmarkt

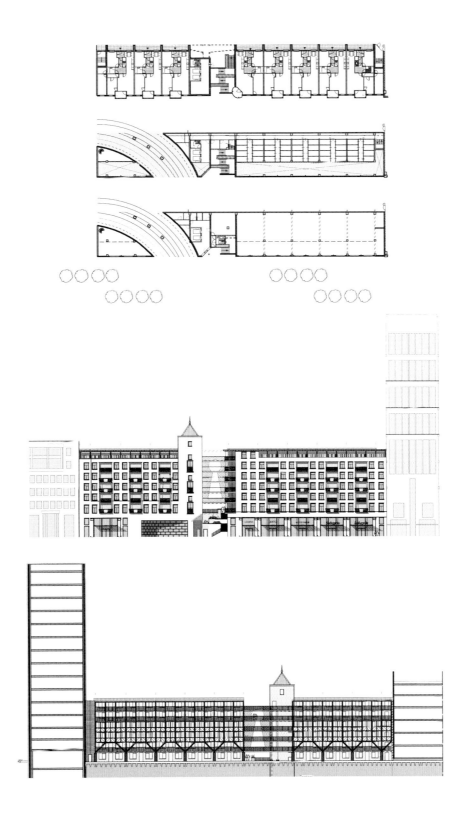

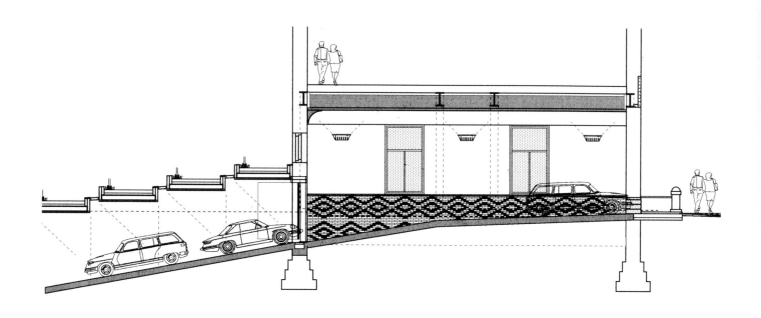

left page: main entrance parking, Fluwelen Burgwal
right page: former freemasons' lodge,
bottom left: ground floor plan, bottom right: floor plan

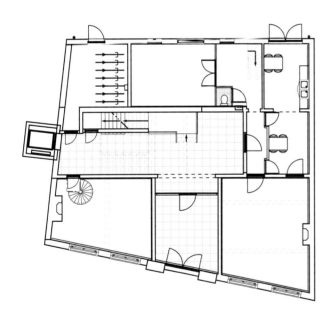

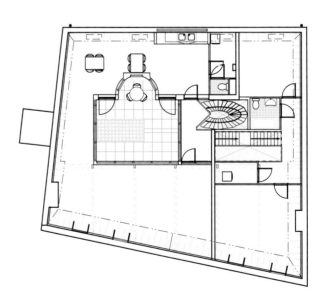

Michael Graves

Michael Graves, Gary Lapera

33,400 square metres of office space
Parnassusplein–Zwarteweg

Are there any rules governing architecture? Indeed there are; countless books full of rules and tips have been written over the course of the centuries. Yet it seems as if architects' work only becomes really interesting when they have acquired sufficient self-confidence to break the rules. Usually such breaches of the rules are rapidly encapsulated in a new scholastic system and then milked for all they are worth until they eventually expire. The history of the Modern Movement is an all too familiar example of this process. Architects permanently in search of adventure are rare but they do exist: Claude-Nicolas Ledoux, H.P. Berlage and Michael Graves belong to this select company. Quatremère de Quincy, the king of architectural rulemaking in Ledoux's time, accused the latter of subjecting architecture to 'a species of torture'.

Michael Graves belongs to the generation who began their careers when the scholastic system of the Modern Movement was in full flower but already beginning to show the first signs of canker. Like the other members of the New York Five, Graves initially tried to resolve this problem by submitting scholasticism to a kind of analytical radicalization. The true master in this field, however, was Peter Eisenman. Graves had always shown a propensity for undisciplined behaviour, a penchant for colour and a certain leaning towards architectural extravagance that was out of step with analytical severity. During the 1970s his work became increasingly mutinous until, in 1980, the Portland Building made it clear once and for all that Graves had embarked on a revolutionary undertaking.

The well-known series of studies for the façade of the Portland Building is a kind of exercise in breaking the rules, both old and new, with a view to breathing new life into the inevitable box-like shape of contemporary office buildings. Graves's design for The Resident was also preceded by a series of preliminary studies. From the outset it was clear that the essence of the design problem lay in the top of the building, or the roof.

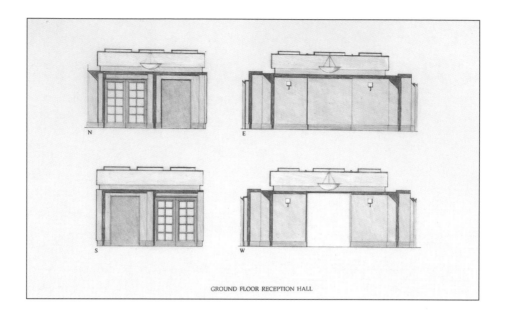

GROUND FLOOR RECEPTION HALL

Several of these early sketches show a projecting top, vaguely reminiscent of Ernesto Rogers's Torre Velasca in Milan. In the end Graves opted for the most low-key, and consequently for the Netherlands the most appropriate, concept: a top consisting of two tall but simple saddleback roofs.

The end result is a fairly large office building suggestive of an Amsterdam canal house that has been touched by the magic wand of a giant order. People may dismiss this invention as an 'architectural joke' if they wish, but it is in fact a synthesis of the Dutch dwelling, a classicist approach to the problem of scale, and the programmatic requirements of a modern office building. A future observer will be able to make some interesting comparisons of architectural approaches to large volumes in the immediate vicinity of Graves's building. Richard Meier, Rob Krier, Cesar Pelli and Sjoerd Soeters all demonstrate that there are other ways of doing it. Yet in this exciting ensemble of office colossi it seems as if it is Graves who shows the way, as if a sophisticated sense of irony is after all the most appropriate response to the problems of our times.

top left: ground floor reception hall
top right: typical floor plan
bottom right: ground floor plan

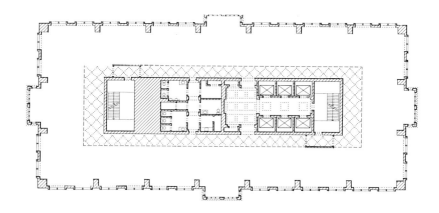

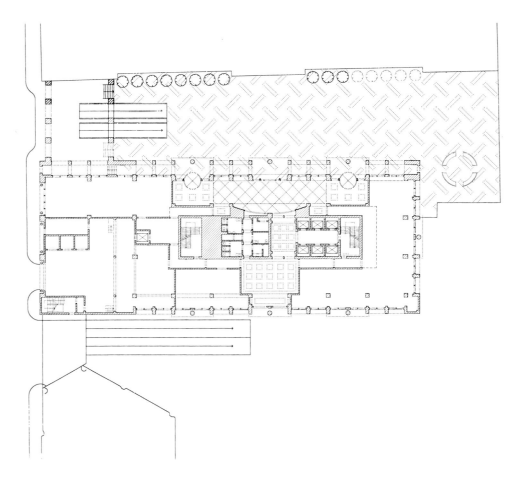

Transitorium
End elevation
Gram

Transition
Zwarteweg elevation

Karelse Van der Meer Architecten

36 apartments
Calliopestraat

Thon Karelse and his partner Jurjen van der Meer have built up a remarkable oeuvre over the past ten years. Young Dutch architects do not have an easy time of it, for the great tradition of Dutch modernism is an onerous legacy. With predecessors of the likes of H.P. Berlage, J.J.P. Oud, Jan Duiker and Gerrit Rietveld, the drawing board is fraught with inhibitions. In Dutch housing construction in particular 'classic' modernism was progressively watered down during the 1960s and 1970s into a product which, though it could be produced cheaply and in quantity, had ceased to have anything in common with the great buildings of the pre-war period.

The generation faced with the task of breathing new life into Dutch modernism in the early 1980s had to reverse this process and turn a mass product back into architecture. In this they succeeded wonderfully well and the resulting architecture has been dubbed 'modernism without dogma' by the critic Hans Ibelings. Its proponents frequently resorted to colour and material to add spice to the bland pap of housing construction. Yet the observant spectator also noted the emergence of a new qualitative standard, for the most persuasive work was produced by those architectural offices who were most sparing in their application of this new festivity. Karelse and Van der Meer are unquestionably among the top practitioners of this restrained genre. Their buildings are characterized by a highly distinguished elegance that has more to do with the quality of the 'cut' than with gratuitous embellishments.

The two apartment blocks in The Resident, on either side of Calliopestraat, show that the design of good quality dwellings – quite properly one of the traditional concerns of Dutch modernism – is in good hands with Karelse and Van der Meer. Nevertheless, there is one striking difference between the Calliopestraat design and their other housing projects. As a rule these designers conform to the modernist demand for 'honest' design,

meaning that they do not eschew repetition – after all, housing is all about a number of identical dwellings. Consequently, Thon Karelse, the designer for this project, started off by drawing two fairly abstract façades for The Resident, façades that were entirely appropriate for a modern apartment building.

Leaving aside their intrinsic quality, these façades simply did not mesh with Rob Krier's idea that Calliopestraat development should be attuned to the smaller scale of the adjacent historic city centre. After a few skirmishes with the supervisors, Karelse eventually bowed to the requirements of the development plan. His final design reveals two 'street façades' with all the appearance of traditional lot development. Even the distribution of windows in the façade surface and the shape of the window frames are reminiscent of the traditional urban dwelling – a typical example of the 'school of lies' according to true modernist orthodoxy. Nonetheless, it is hard to deny that the result is especially charming. Calliopestraat could well become a very popular little residential street and if that should happen it will prove that residents are quite capable of appreciating architecture that takes an occasional liberty with truth.

top right: floor plan
bottom right: ground floor plan

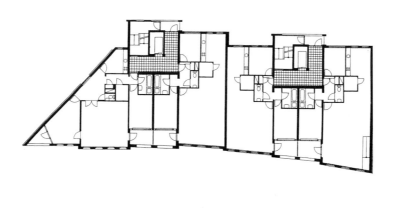

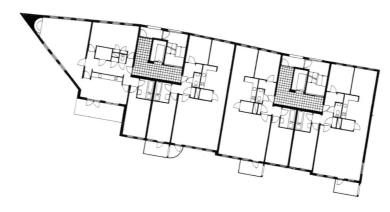

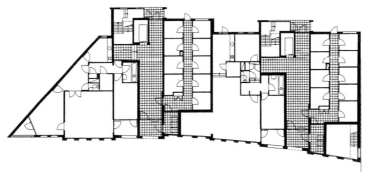

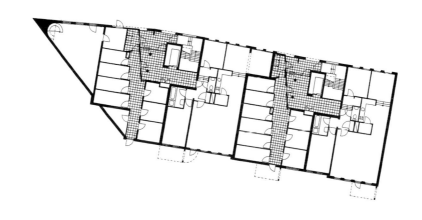

top left: façade Calliopestraat, northern block
bottom left: back façade Calliopestraat, northern block
top right: façade Calliopestraat, southern block
bottom right: back façade Calliopestraat, southern block

Rob Krier

7,800 square metres of office space
Muzentoren

4,700 square metres of office space
Fluwelen Burgwal corner
3,600 square metres office space

135 square metres of retail space
Turfmarkt corner

This book has already had quite a lot to say about the urbanist Rob Krier, but there is also an architect called Rob Krier. One gets the impression that the radical anti-modernism of the urbanist is applied somewhat less rigorously by the architect. The reasons for this are probably of a more practical than theoretical nature. In his book on architectural composition, Krier demonstrates his considerable knowledge of the architecture of earlier times yet precisely because of this he knows, probably better than most, that the modern practice of building is so different from the old craftsmanly tradition that it makes no sense for an architect to design seriously historicized buildings. Even restoration projects run up against this problem.

Krier's built works, which include a lot of housing projects in Berlin, show what is possible in practice. In his composition, Krier often succeeds in coming close to the wealth of forms so characteristic of the past. Sometimes his façades are reminiscent of Loos, sometimes of the superb turn-of-the-century Berlin apartment blocks; some are stuccoed, others are in brick, but the relation of wall surface to window openings is always exciting. Krier avoids problems with the budget and the imperative of rapid, mechanized construction by keeping the detailing very sober. This tends to be overlooked at first sight because the viewer's attention is seized by the overall composition. So inured have we become to the monotonous repetition of window openings, both horizontally and vertically, that any hint of poetry in this area is an occasion for joy.

The ensemble of buildings that Krier has designed for The Resident demonstrate once again that with relatively sober detailing and a thoughtful composition, he is capable of producing striking but nonetheless feasible results. The tower element, that is flanked by two other sections both of which form the head of a building block, was in itself a highly unusual design project. For a designer like Krier, for whom urbanism

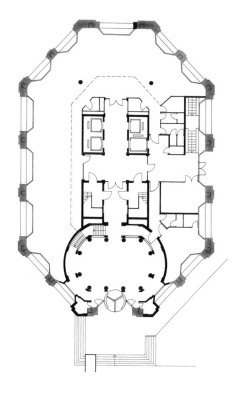
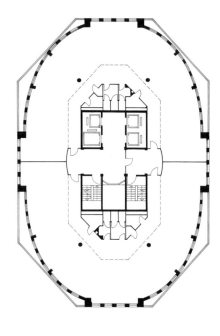

and architecture are indissoluble, it offered the opportunity of reviving the old concept of civic art.

The two flanking sections enabled Krier to place the Muzentoren within a perfect frame. In so doing he opted for a subtle form of asymmetry, for despite their many similarities, the flanking sections are not mirror images. The symmetry of the tower itself serves to anchor the composition as a whole, and total symmetry – as Ruskin well knew – would have proved fatal. The cityscape coalesces in the articulation of the tower. The axis of the building – and that of the square behind it – is accentuated by a narrow, high and dominating façade element that connects, both horizontally and vertically, the various components of the composition. In the vertical articulation a clear distinction has been made between the part of the tower that belongs to the urban space and the part that rises above it. The fact that the tower will be executed in an almost black brick is just the finishing touch in an already highly dramatic ensemble of buildings.

top left: ground floor plan and floor plan Muzen-toren
top right: ground floor plan and floor plan head Turfmarkt
bottom right: ground floor plan and floor plan head Fluwelen Burgwal

126

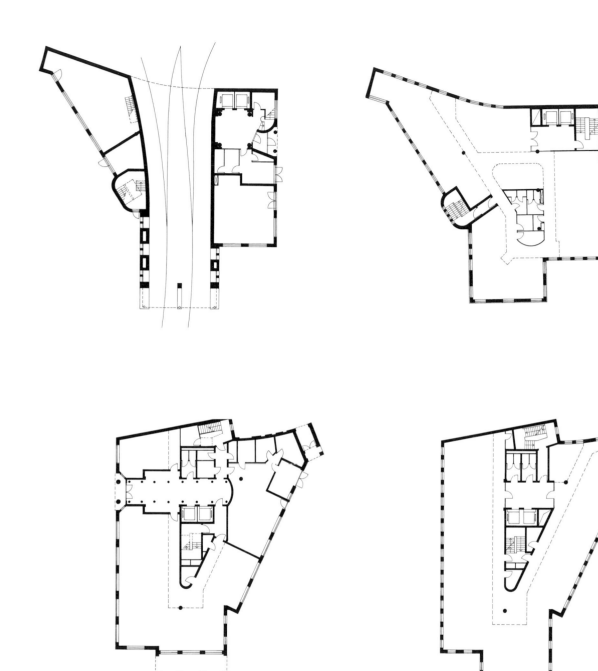

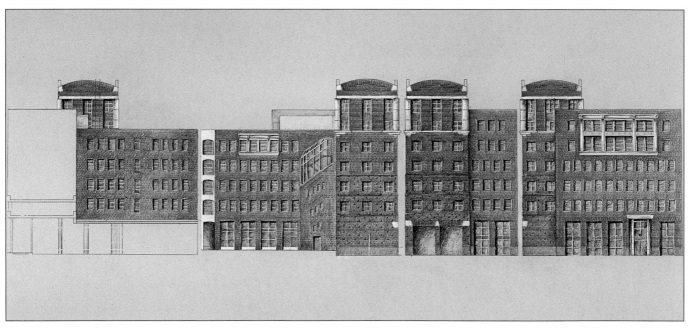

top left: façades head Turfmarkt
bottom left: façades head Fluwelen Burgwal

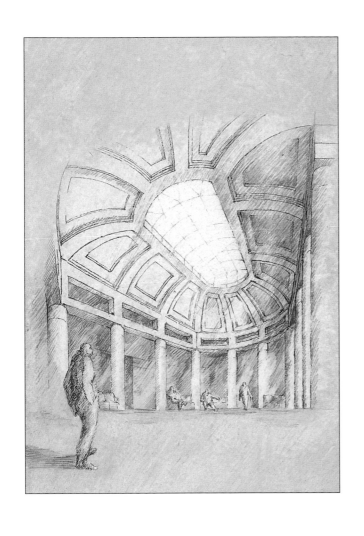

Adolfo Natalini

Adolfo Natalini, Corinne Schrauwen

169 apartments, 455 square metres of retail space
Clioplein-Muzenplein

Adolfo Natalini is a very versatile architect. He began his career with Superstudio, an office dedicated mainly to the production of 'architettura radicale': surrealistic-utopian designs for 'continuous monuments' that reveal a kind of urbanism on a world scale. Also famous is his series of villa designs, dated 1968–1970, where a rigid grid enforces a strictly rational analysis. The same approach, applied to furniture design, resulted in the commercially successful 'Misura' series. It was with this work that Natalini made a strong showing at the 1973 Milan Triennial organized by Aldo Rossi.

During the 1970s Natalini, like Michael Graves, tired of the possibilities offered by analytical rationalism. A plan for a museum building in Frankfurt, presented in 1980, exhibited distinct stylistic allusions to German architecture of the 1900–1930 period. At the same time Natalini designed and built two other buildings, one in Como and one in Bologna, which, while they were not so explicitly historicist, nonetheless marked his permanent return to traditional architectural themes. In the course of the 1980s Natalini once again demonstrated the versatility of his talent with a series of superb town square designs, as for instance in Palazzuolo sul Senio. These piazzas show that, after a flying start with avant-garde architecture, Natalini had also succeeded in mastering the secrets of tradition, both in architecture and urban design, down to the smallest detail.

The design brief for The Resident was more or less tailor-made for Natalini: a housing development that would provide the 'walls' of two small, typically urban squares, executed in brick. On Muzenplein he has tried to achieve a visual reduction of the building height by setting back the top two storeys. Combined with the arcade around the square, which is also two storeys high, this produces a powerful illusion of small-scale development: no mean feat considering that the buildings around the square are seven storeys high. As

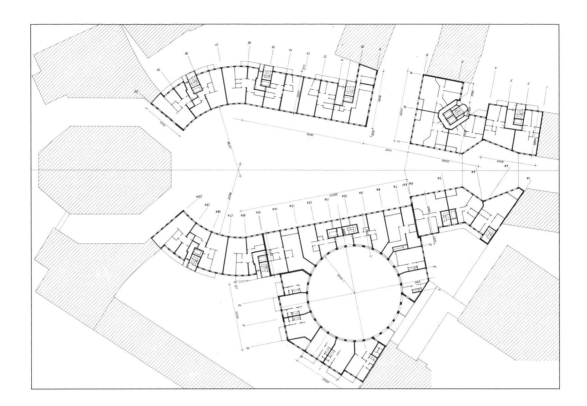

a result of the façade design, in particular the deep reveals, the wall surfaces around the square are so de-materialized that the relatively small space involved here seems to be bounded by a screen of narrow window piers. The visual accents are provided by three towers that together form an odd kind of asymmetrical balance along the axis of the square. Krier's tall office towers, which are seen against the sun, will always appear as a dark mass; Natalini's two smaller residential towers on the other side of the square are much more strongly lit but their scale is reduced by Graves's and Pelli's high-rise seen in the background. For the aficionado Muzenplein promises to be a striking urban panorama.

The neighbouring Clioplein has a very different, and above all subdued, character. The restrained architectural design here recalls the inside of the traditional perimeter block. Although this square, too, is public, it has more of a 'neighbourhood' quality, like the squares in the old quarters of the city in the days before there was such a thing as through traffic.

left: fourth floor plan
top right: first floor plan
bottom right: ground floor plan

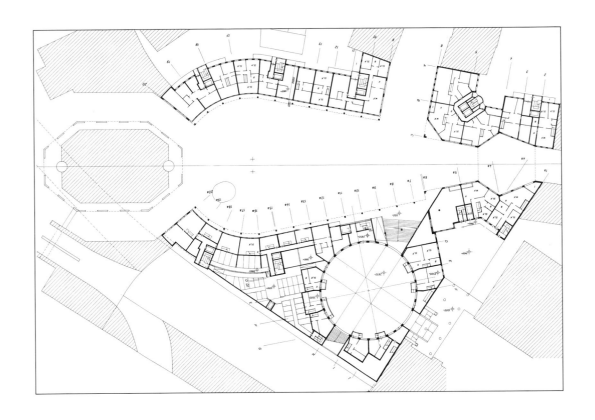

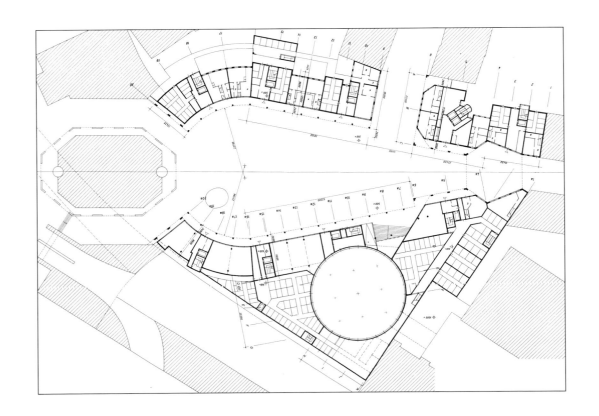

133

22.1

+20825

+20050

+17400

+14700

+12000

+9300

+6600

+3900

+2650

Cesar Pelli

Cesar Pelli, Fred Clarke

23,110 square metres of office space
Muzenstraat–Zwarteweg

Cesar Pelli, born in 1926, is the oldest member of the team of architects who designed The Resident; at the same time he is one of the last representatives of the Modern Movement. His entire oeuvre is characterized by an increasingly firm command of the stylistic resources introduced during the 1950s for the design of large office buildings. As Pelli has demonstrated, the structural element of the load-bearing frame with its enveloping curtain wall need not lead to a bland, grey box. The articulation of the volume and the detailing of the façade continue to offer new possibilities for ringing the changes. Colour and the classic feature of the setback evidently provide an experienced designer like Pelli with seemingly endless ways of solving a recurrent design task.

The odd thing about Pelli's towers is that some of them not only rise upwards, like all tall buildings, but also flow downwards, from top to base, in an awesome cascade. The curtain wall of the residential tower block above the Museum of Modern Art in New York looks like a frozen waterfall and the Norwest Center in Minneapolis reminds one of the thunderous natural violence of Niagara Falls. It is as if Pelli is intent on visualizing the finely balanced tension between gravity on the one hand and the opposing structural violence of the frame on the other hand: the façade between base and top becomes the outward expression of a force field.

Compared with the Norwest Center, the office building Pelli has designed for The Resident is a midget. Nonetheless, the various developmental stages reveal that here, too, Pelli has sought to invest his design of the volume with an element of tension. As the study models make clear, a delicate top combined with a slight emphasis on vertical lines can make a relatively low and potentially squat tower look surprisingly slim. It is in this context that the importance of the detailing becomes evident. As a functional-

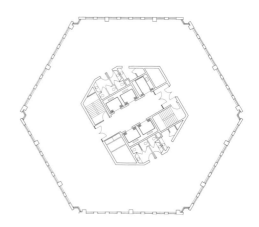

ist, albeit a very sophisticated one, Pelli seeks to visualize each floor of a building and to show that, structurally speaking, façades are no more than a skin. The result is a complex play of lines that must be expressed in the brickwork, including the right colour joint.

The final design is an almost fairytale marriage that demonstrates, in the final moments of the century, that a reconciliation between Amsterdam School and avant-garde architecture is possible. At the time, around 1930 and again in the 1950s, this seemed completely out of the question, and consequently the creative use of brick quietly died out in the Netherlands. It is ironic that it should have been left to an American in The Hague to show that the deep division in Dutch architectural history is based on a misunderstanding. In Cesar Pelli's design, Michel de Klerk and Jan Duiker shake hands posthumously. The controversy that raged in their day seems – in retrospect – incomprehensible. The much-criticized 'apron architecture' of the Amsterdam School was in fact nothing but a curtain wall, as are all the old Amsterdam street façades. The witch hunt against the attempt to impart a modicum of expression to these brick façades is quite unfathomable today. As H.P. Berlage foresaw in the late 1920s, the fundamental rejection of every form of decoration, even when it involved the relatively austere articulation of large façade surfaces, was a form of radicalism that was bound to come to no good.

top left: typical floor plan
bottom left: façade corner Muzenstraat–Zwarteweg
top right: ground floor plan
bottom right: façade Muzenstraat

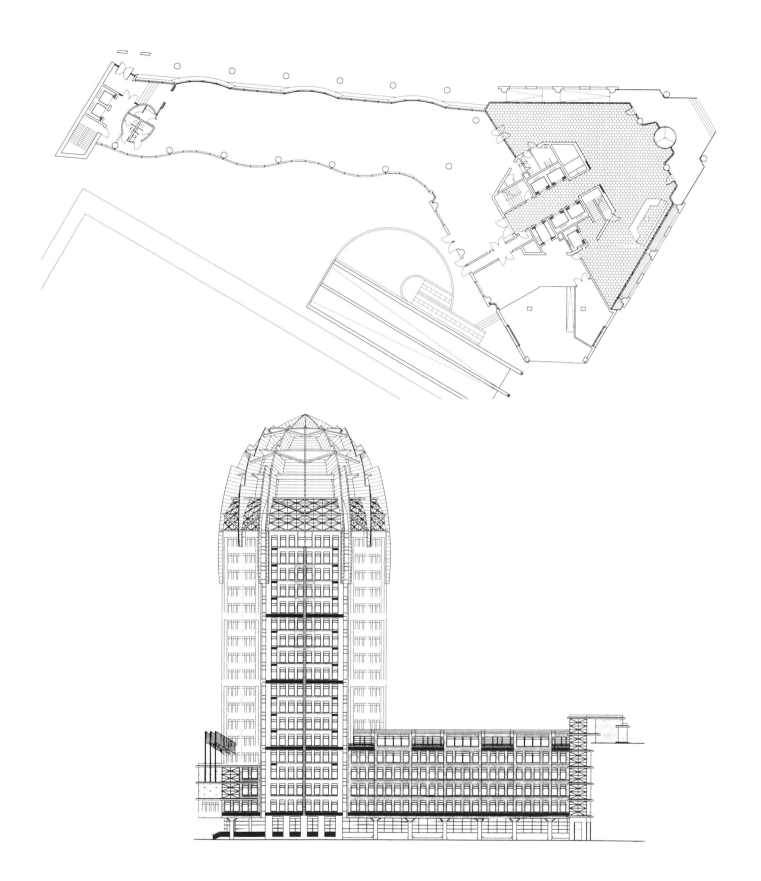

Sjoerd Soeters

Sjoerd Soeters, Jos van Eldonk

29,000 square metres of office space
1,900 square metres of retail space
230 parking slots
Turfmarkt–Zwarteweg

Self-willed, an excellent but little-used adjective, describes Sjoerd Soeters to a T; he is a self-willed architect. While many of his contemporaries have sought a cautious compromise between the unrelenting austerity of post-war Dutch modernism and the new desire for a less self-effacing approach to architecture, Soeters has gone in brazen pursuit of maximum festivity. There's no accounting for taste, as the saying goes, but that has never prevented a veritable army of know-alls from trying to determine what 'good taste' is. Soeters's work often testifies to a sovereign disdain for the colourless respectability that usually passes for good taste.

The interior of his own house on the Amsterdam Prinsengracht is a superb early example of Soeterian rococo – and pure anathema to functionalist-inclined arbiters of taste. A more recent example is the gambling hall in Zandvoort which seems to be all frills, furbelows and slot machines; the design has been denounced as 'a boy's dream run amok'. In his defence, Soeters himself tends to cite American examples - Las Vegas, of course, and the interior decoration that turns many hotels on both sides of the Atlantic into a breathtaking experience. Nevertheless, European architecture history can boast a similar tendency, namely expressionism. It produced Hans Poelzig's Grosses Schauspielhaus in Berlin, to name a German example, and of course the work, and especially the interiors, of the Amsterdam School.

The accumulation of detail that generally characterizes the work of Amsterdam School does not sit well on large buildings. The Scheepvaarthuis in Amsterdam demonstrates more or less where its limits lie; for the Bijenkorf department store in The Hague, Piet Kramer developed a quite different syntax. Similarly, Soeters's design for The Resident shows that such a huge office complex can have a sobering effect on even an incorrigible devotee of extravagance like Soeters. The various development stages of the design illustrate

façade Zwarteweg

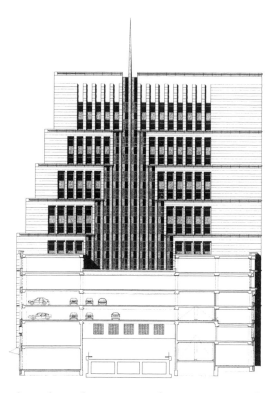

how the architect's quest for expressionist drama kept getting bogged down in a profusion of detailing. The datum of 30,000 square metres of office space, shops and a car park was not amenable to sheer formal ambition. The logic of the building task and the force of the required volume were enough to bring even the most passionate of fabulists down to earth.

In the end Soeters managed to find the right balance between the building programme and his pursuit of a strongly individual form. The view is dominated by the three vertical slabs with the tram tunnel providing the dramatic interest. The lower section, containing the street façade on Turfmarkt, plays a secondary role in the composition. The observant spectator will perceive a slight emphasis on the complex accumulation of functions in this horizontal section, but in the main Soeters has wisely decided to confine himself to the broad lines of the plan. The other side of the building, on Parnassusplein, is also dominated by the vertical sections, but here Soeters has seized on the fact that stairs and lifts can be architecturally accentuated, so that the three office slabs appear surprisingly slender and tall.

top right: typical floor plan
middle right: fourth floor plan
bottom: ground floor plan

146

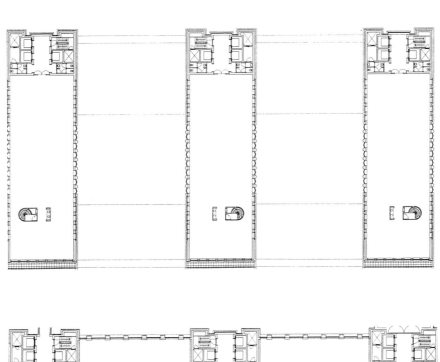

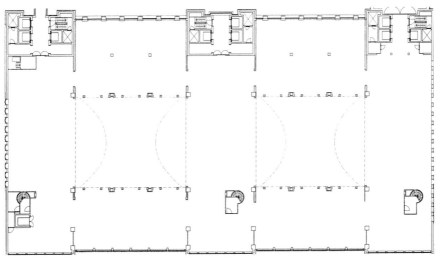

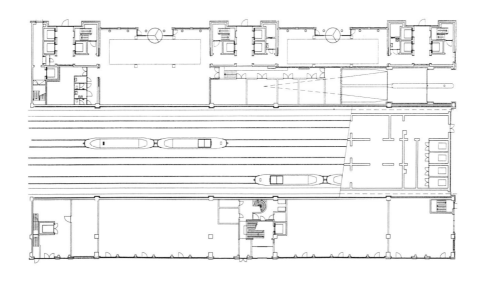

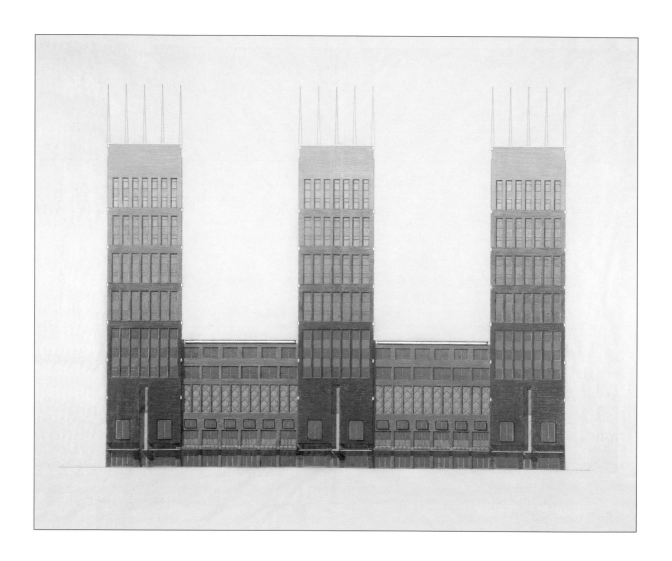

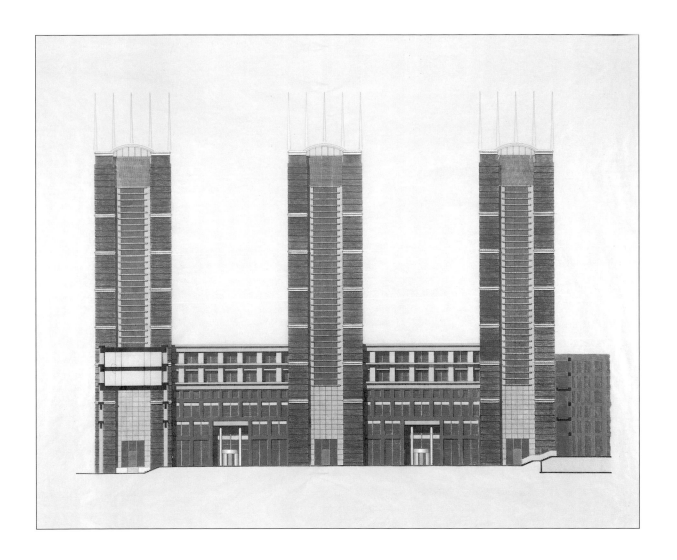

left: façade Turfmarkt
right: façade Parnassusplein

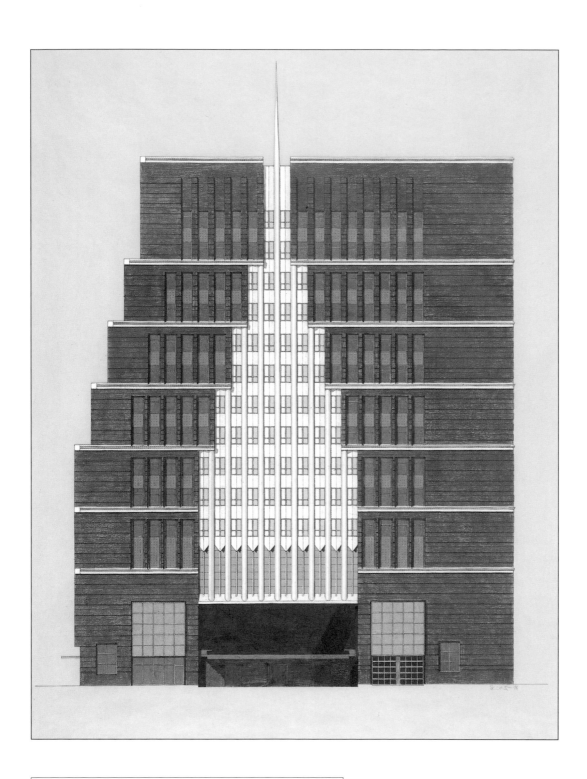

façade Zwarteweg

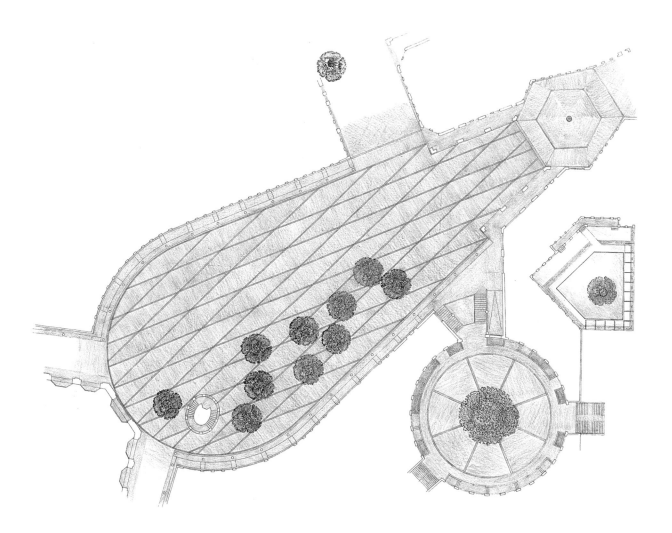

CH & Partners

Design for the urban space

The Resident comprises a great many urban spaces of widely varying character. In a sense this was precisely what Rob Krier intended: a richly varied cityscape such as one finds in old European cities. Thus the master plan reveals three squares, four courtyards and two narrow streets bordered by high buildings – the sort of street profiles that are found only in historic town centres.

On the master plan these areas appear as blanks, for such spaces still have to be 'furnished' in much the same way as a house has to be furnished once the architect has done his job. Indeed, Berlage referred to the function of city squares in terms of 'banquet halls for the citizenry'. Frank Cardinaal and Richard Koek, in collaboration with the City of The Hague, have come up with a development plan that is ardently low-key. The paving used in all the urban spaces – brick ranging in colour from brown to slate grey – alludes to the Binnenhof and hence indirectly to a Dutch tradition. On Muzenplein this paving is enriched with a diagonal pattern of twelve-centimetre-wide lines executed in freestone. Only the (provisionally) semi-public Parnassusplein will look different – a little less neutral perhaps – because this narrow space between two very tall buildings can do with an additional accent or two.

The Resident does not offer much opportunity for planting mature trees. The scale of Krier's streets and squares, which have an urban, or rather town-centre intimacy, is such that large, dense tree crowns would simply produce too much shade. The designers consequently opted for the acacia, a species of tree with delicate, translucent foliage. However, the future inhabitants of The Resident will find most of the greenery concentrated behind their dwellings, in typical enclosed town gardens. Here, too, the possibilities for planting are limited but at least they are ensured the smell of damp vegetation and earth after a summer evening thunderstorm. In such contexts, even a single honeysuckle can be enormously enriching.

Muzenplein and Clioplein

It is of course impossible to look at the urban space in The Resident in isolation from the surrounding development, which is to say the old Hague city centre. Herengracht is obviously a superb amenity and Turfmarkt, were it to be lavishly planted with trees, might become a genuine boulevard. Fluwelen Burgwal is in desperate need of a facelift, which it will get, and the same applies to Zwarteweg on the eastern side of the planning area. Kees Rijnboutt, Joan Busquets and the City of The Hague are jointly responsible for the development of this typically Hague ensemble. Given that all involved are resolved to achieve the best possible result, it looks as if the public space in and around The Resident will be able to bear comparison with historic examples.

154

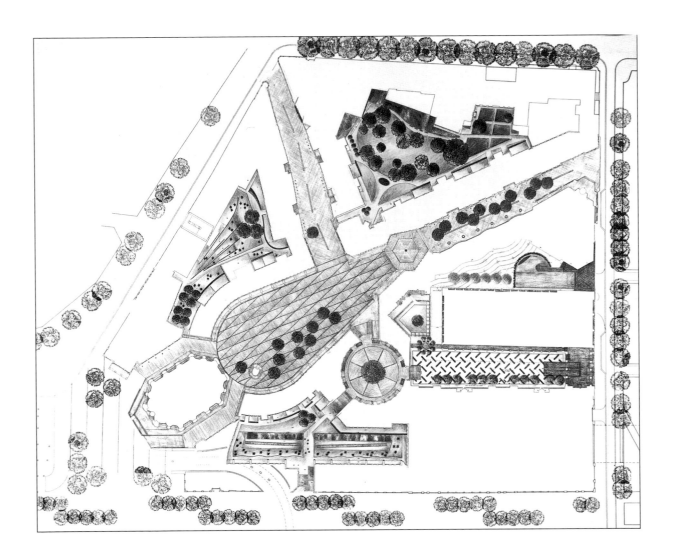

development plan

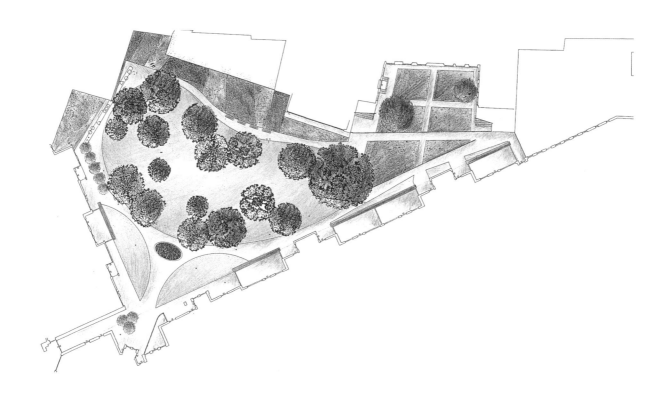

left: Herengracht garden
top right: Fluwelen garden
bottom right: Clio-garden

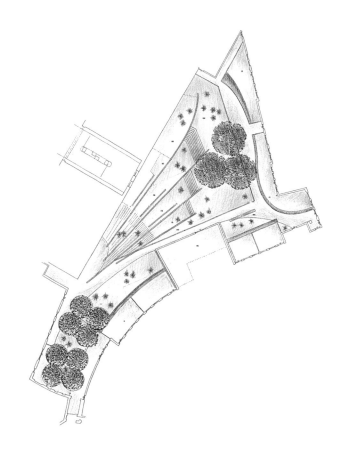

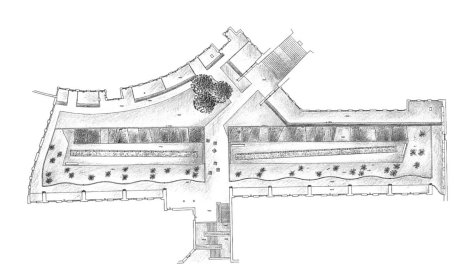

Personal Index

Aymonino, Carlo 25
Alberti, Leon Battista 29
Alexander, Christopher 21
Argan, Carlo 21

Bakema, Jaap 20, 23, 24
Banham, Reyner 12, 22, 23, 24, 26
Baumeister, Reinhard 38, 39
Behrendt, Walter Curt 40
Behrens, Peter 17, 22
Benevolo, Leonardo 26
Berlage, H.P. 17, 25, 33, 36, 39, 40, 41, 44, 45, 46, 47, 48, 49, 55, 64, 68, 70, 91, 113, 119, 140, 153
Bosse, Mieke 80
Brinckmann, A.E. 14, 33
Broek, J.H. van den 48
Brunelleschi, Filippo 29
Busquets, Joan 89, 154

Cardinaal, Frank 89, 90, 153
Carlo, Giancarlo de 23
Clarke, Fred 139
Colenbrander, Bernard 91, 92
Cuypers, P.J.H. 28

Daan, Gunnar 63, 74, 80, 81, 97, 98
Dijk, Hans van 93
Dirrix, Bert 63, 75, 80, 81, 103, 104, 107
Drijver, Peter 63, 71, 77, 80, 107, 108
Dudok, W.M. 46, 47, 48, 49, 52
Duiker, Jan 119, 140
Duivesteijn, Adri 51, 52, 54, 57, 58, 61, 67

Eesteren, Cornelis van 16, 18, 20, 48, 63
Eisenman, Peter 24, 25, 113
Eldonk, Jos van 145
Evers, Frans 6, 62

Eyck, Aldo van 16, 18, 20, 88

Feenstra, G. 39
Fehl, Gerhard 36, 38, 39
Finetti, Giuseppe de 22
Foster, Norman 58

Gabetti, Roberto 23
Gardella, Ignazio 23
Gessner, Albert 40
Giedion, Sigfried 18, 26
Graaf, W.A. de 46
Grabowsky & Poort 67, 78, 81, 87
Graves, Michael 25, 29, 69, 76, 79, 82, 83, 84, 86, 87, 92, 113, 114, 131, 132

Haussmann, G.E. 44, 103
Hejduk, John 25
Henrici, Karl 38
Hertzberger, Herman 54
Horsefall, T.C. 39
Hosper, Alle 89
Hulshoff 46
Huxtable, Ada Louise 83

Ibelings, Hans 119
Isola, Aimaro 23

Kahn, Albert 87
Karelse, Thon 74, 80, 81, 82, 119, 120
Keppler, Arie 40, 41
Klerk, Michel de 41, 140
Koek, Richard 89, 90, 153
Kramer, Piet 90, 145
Krier, Leon 25
Krier, Rob 5, 6, 25, 30, 31, 32, 33, 34, 35, 36, 38, 58, 59, 60, 61, 63, 64, 65, 66, 68, 69, 70, 71, 72, 73, 74, 75, 76, 77, 78, 79, 80, 81, 82, 84, 87, 89, 92, 93, 103, 107, 114, 120, 125, 126, 139, 153
Kropholler, A.J. 46

Lampugnani, Vittorio 34, 36, 38
Lapera, Gary 87
Le Corbusier 9, 10, 12, 13, 18, 20, 22, 26, 27, 83, 97
Ledoux, C.N. 113
Leeuw, C.H. van der 92
Loos, Adolf 22, 23, 25, 125
Lynch, Kevin 21

Mackintosh, Charles Rennie 23
Mebes, Paul 40
Meer, Jurjen van der 80, 119
Meier, Richard 55, 83, 114
Meijer, Ton 6, 58, 69, 71
Messel, Alfred 40
Meyer, Haiko 81
Mies van der Rohe, Ludwig 35
Mitscherlich, Alexander 14, 19
Mondriaan, P. 82
Mordaunt Crook, J. 93
Mumford, Lewis 13, 15, 16, 19, 26
Muthesius, Hermann 23
Muzio, Giovanni 22

Natalini, Adolfo 25, 29, 69, 75, 76, 77, 78, 79, 81, 84, 88, 131, 132
Nijpels, Ed 61
Noordanus, Peter 6, 61, 63, 69, 79, 80, 89

Oud, J.J.P. 92, 93, 98, 119

Palladio, Andrea 26, 84
Pehnt, Wolfgang 35, 36
Pelli, Cesar 16, 69, 75, 76, 79, 80, 82, 83, 84, 87, 114, 132, 139, 140
Perret, Auguste 17, 22, 24, 97, 103, 104
Pevsner, Nikolaus 26
Picasso, Pablo 23
Plecnik, Josef 90
Poelzig, Hans 145
Posener, Julius 34, 38
Pugin, A.W.N. 28

Quatremère de Quincy, A.C. 113
Quist, Wim 54

Rietveld, Gerrit 28, 119
Rijnboutt, Kees 61, 63, 65, 66, 69, 71, 80, 91, 92, 154
Rogers, Ernesto 22, 23, 24, 114
Rossi, Aldo 24, 25, 27, 29, 30, 84, 131
Rowe, Colin 26, 27, 28, 29, 34, 35
Ruijssenaars, Hans 57, 59, 72
Ruskin, John 126

Saarinen, Eero 16
Samonà, Giuseppe 22
Schinkel, Friedrich 35, 36, 38
Schrauwen, Corinne 131
Schultze-Naumburg, Paul 38, 39
Sitte, Camillo 34, 38, 39, 40
Sluys, F. van der 76
Soeters, Sjoerd 63, 69, 76, 78, 80, 84, 85, 86, 87, 89, 114, 145, 146
Stirling, James 9, 10, 12, 35, 36
Stübben, Joseph 39

Tafuri, Manfredo 22, 24, 25
Taverne, Ed 23
Tijen, W. van 20

Ungers, Mathias 25
Unwin, Raymond 18, 39, 40

Velden, Joop ten 51, 52, 53

Wagner, Otto 23
Weeber, Carel 47, 49, 53, 54, 55, 57, 58, 59, 72, 97
Witteveen, W.G. 92, 93
Wittkower, Rudolf 26
Wright, Frank Lloyd 23, 66, 67

Zevi, Bruno 22

158

Colophon

This publication was made possible through the support of MAB Groep bv, The Hague and through a grant of the Netherlands Fund for Architecture (Stimuleringsfonds voor Architectuur), Rotterdam.

Concept: Vincent van Rossem, Mariet Schoenmakers
Graphic Design: Joseph Plateau, Amsterdam
Printing: Drukkerij Rosbeek bv, Nuth
Binding: Spiegelenberg, Zoetermeer
Translation Dutch-English: Robyn de Jong-Dalziel
Visual materials: Ingrid Oosterheerd
Production: Astrid Vorstermans
Publisher: Simon Franke

Credits of the illustrations
de Architecten Cie, Amsterdam: page 54, 55
Michel Boesveld, Amsterdam: page 84
Dienst Stedelijke Ontwikkeling, The Hague: page 48, 49, 50, 51, 52, 60
Gilbert Fastenaekens, Brussels: page 102 (up)
Fondation Le Corbusier, Paris/o SPADEM: page 8, 10, 10-11
Ezra Stoller, Esto, New York: page 11
Rob Krier, Vienna/Berlin: page 30-31, 32, 33, 37 (top right)
MAB Groep bv, The Hague: page 65 (bottom), 68, 69, 72-78, 80-83, 85-88
NAi, Collectie, Rotterdam: page 14-15, 24, 34, 37 (bottom right), 40, 41, 42, 47
Carlo Palazzolo and Riccardo Vio, published in: Carlo Palazzolo and Riccardo Vio (editors), *Sulle tracce di Le Corbusier*, Venice 1989. Courtesy Arsenale Editrice, Venice: page 9
Rijksgebouwendienst, The Hague: page 56, 59, 63, 64, 65 (top)
Hans Ruijssenaars, Amsterdam: page 70
Ingrid Oosterheerd, Amsterdam: page 91
Ger van der Vlugt, Amsterdam: page 90
All other illustrations (page 96-157): MAB and the architects

ISBN 90-5662-013-4

Printed and Bound in the Netherlands

Available in North, South and Central America through D.A.P./Distributed Art Publishers 636 Broadway, 12th floor, New York, NY 10012, Tel. 212 473-5119 Fax 212 673-2887